MW00365817

In praise of

'BEHAVE – What To Do When Your Child Won't'

"The book flows well and is easy to read. I like the combination of narrative and dialogue and I enjoyed the signpost and cartoon images. A relevant, helpful, practical resource for parents at all stages of their parenting journey."
Marie Reilly, Dublin

"I would highly recommend this book to all parents as a resource when they are challenged to think of helpful ways to interact with their children. It is an easy read with a very powerful message about family wellbeing and the value of peer support for parents."
Cathy Lynch (mother)

"I've just finished your excellent parenting book. I love the tone, the informal approach and how it works into the teaching element."
Aileen Rogers, Founder of 'Ready Girls'

"Behaviour - kids, parents? This fantastic book helps us to understand the fine balance between their behaviour & ours, and how to deal with challenging family / daily situations"
Olivia, Mum of three

You can follow news, updates and discussion about this book by using the hashtag #BEHAVEbook   For more information visit http://**www.behave.ie**

About the Author

Val Mullally
is a Parenting Expert and Relationship Coach who is passionate about supporting parents to create more enjoyable and fulfilling family life. She and her husband have adult children and are grandparents.

Val is an experienced teacher and principal and wishes she'd discovered the secrets in this book when her kids were young, because she has seen how these tools and insights can transform family life.

Val is Founder of Koemba Parent Coaching.
Follow her on twitter on **@valmullally**

All Facebook 'likes' appreciated. :)
https://www.facebook.com/Koemba

Val is available as a Keynote Speaker and as a Relationship Coach.

For more about Val and her online Parenting Courses see:

www.koemba.com   Contact Val at **val@koemba.com**

Foreword

I've known Val Mullally a few years now and have been waiting with baited breath for her book, 'BEHAVE - What To Do When Your Child Won't'. Not only is Val a parenting expert and AC accredited coach but, much more than that, she is a passionate teacher that inspires parents to be the best they can be. Her wisdom and encouragement has been translated into a book that is useful to every parent; a book with clear signposts and helpful, practical tools to guide parents in a non-judgmental, positive way.

Through a combination of real-life stories and easy-to-follow techniques, Val's book tackles parenting challenges by enabling the reader to look at the wider dynamics of each situation. She encourages parents to perceive 'bad behavior' as an opportunity to strengthen relationships and create a co-operative, connected family environment.

If you are looking for a quick-fix that enables you to control your child's behavior, then this is not the book for you. If you seek a mindful long-term approach to parenting that builds your child's self-esteem and supports their inherent ability to make positive decisions, this will be your bible.

Billie Browne, Founder & Editor, Oh Baby! Magazine, Ireland

BEHAVE
What To Do When Your Child Won't

Val Mullally

Whilst this book is designed to give helpful tips and insights to Parents, the advice and strategies may not be suitable for every situation. This book is not a substitute for advice from a trained coach, counsellor or therapist. If you are concerned that yourself, your child or your family require expert advice or assistance, it is of primary importance for you to seek the services of a competent professional who deals with such concerns.

First published in the Republic of Ireland in 2015.

Copyright © 2015 by Valerie Joy Mullally
All rights reserved. This book, or parts thereof, may not be reproduced in any form without written permission of the copyright owner.

Mullally, Val
Koemba Publications
BEHAVE - What To Do When Your Child Won't
For contact details see www.behave.ie
Twitter: @valmullally hashtag: #BEHAVEbook

ISBN: 9780957176515 (paperback edition)

The characters and incidents in this book are fictional, although they attempt to capture the typical scenarios that many parents experience.

Illustrator: Patrick Fawcett
Design by John Canty - www.johncantydesigner.com

♡

To Dad

"No such word as 'can't'."

Acknowledgements

This book would never have been born without the input of very many different people. To every child who has influenced me - my own children, grandchildren, 'adopted' grandchildren, family and friends' children, pupils and even those whose fleeting encounter left an impression, I thank you.

To my father, now no longer in this world, who lived his belief in God, provided a secure home in my growing years, and who taught me 'no such word as can't'; and to my patient, loving mother, you have always been great influences in my life.

To my husband Bill - you are the wind beneath my wings.

Thank you especially for the encouragement and support of my family.

Julie Cunningham - you helped me to see the book was already there!

To Patrick Fawcett, Eithne Ring and Liam Lavery - I love the fun, yet sensitive illustrations, that are an integral part of this book. Thank you!

Of course this book only materialised through the team who handled its production. My appreciation to copy editor Mia Gallagher, and to all who proofread and gave feedback. I am especially grateful to loyal friend and talented digital marketing strategist Marie Collins, founder of 'DigiPulse'. Thanks also to all who assisted with marketing, especially talented and patient webmaster Gabriel Merovingi and ever-willing virtual assistant 'Girl Friday', Lara Costello. Heartfelt appreciation to all who have supported in so many roles, including Billie Browne, Founder and Editor of 'Oh Baby!' magazine, Ireland. Although I may never meet some of these people, they made it happen. Thanks also to Brian O'Kane of Oaktree Press, whose wise mentorship was made possible by South Dublin County Enterprise Board.

My apologies to all who have helped whom I have not named. There have been so many who have encouraged and supported, including my Dublin Tweetup friends, and my SmarterPreneur group.

To loved ones who have encouraged me, especially in the moments I doubted, you know who you are - blessings and deep appreciation.

To all whose shoulders I have stood upon - authors, mentors, trainers, lecturers - you gave me a greater and a wider vision, thank you.

I also acknowledge everyone who has supported my work, my blog, books, webinars, recordings, workshops and presentations. The learning we have shared and the feedback you have given inspires me and made this book possible.

Contents

Introduction

Are you parenting a preschooler or are teen years looming on the horizon? Whether home feels like a car smash right now, or things are cruising along, here's your opportunity to create more enjoyable and fulfilling family life.

In this book you'll find helpful tools to get through the tough spots and you'll discover how to maintain healthy family relationships, where there's more fun, more enjoyment, more connection and cooperation. As the parent you're in charge - you are behind the steering wheel. You determine the family's direction and response to whatever lies in front of you.

Do you want a clear vision of the parenting journey ahead? Do you want to discover key parenting insights and skills to confidently handle challenging twists and turns along that road? Parenting is like learning to drive a car - it's much easier to master key skills on a quiet road, than on a furious highway. Whether your child is a preschooler, a preteen or somewhere in between, you can prevent your relationships from spinning out of control. Here's your opportunity to discover how to keep your family life moving safely and smoothly in the direction you want to head.

In the journey of family life, we all face similar frustrations: sibling rivalry, whining, tantrums, homework issues, power struggles, shyness, over-confidence, laziness or not taking responsibility.

You can find any amount of theory about children's challenging behaviour from television, books, the internet and people in your life - but like every other parent, you want to know 'How?' This book will help you figure out what's needed when you want to yell at your children to 'BEHAVE!'

Whether you are a new or an experienced parent, together we'll unlock some amazingly simple insights and tools to understand children's behaviour and to navigate the road ahead, whatever conditions you face, so that you can create happier family relationships.

As we begin our journey, let's take a peek through Trish's kitchen window. See if you relate to Trish's story:

Supper's on the cooker. Trish glances at her watch. Her daughter Jamie chews her pencil as she tries to figure out her homework.

Trish's mother-in-law is on the other end of the phone, berating the weather, the politicians, the neighbour, the price of her cigarettes now the new tax has been introduced.

'Yes, mmm, uh-huh,' says Trish, half listening. If only Derek would get home.

Baby lets out a roar. Alice is next to him on the mat. Grabbing his teddy. He's not letting go. His little face is crumpled and red, his nose running. Trish puts the phone against her chest to muffle the kids' noise.

'Alice, give it back,' she hisses. Alice doesn't even look her way. She is fixated on the teddy.

'My teddy!' she wails.

'Give it back now!'

Alice flings teddy across the floor. She storms out the room, her high-pitched wail making Trish clench her teeth.

Baby's crying.

'Mary, I need to go. I'll talk later,' Trish ends the call.

'How am I supposed to do my homework!' moans Jamie.

Trish sighs. As she scoops up her little one, who's sobbing for his teddy, Derek comes in the door.

Throughout this book you'll enjoy the highs and lows, the twists and turns of parenting with our typical mum Trish.

As with any road trip, you'll come across signposts. These will guide you on the parenting journey. With Trish, you'll discover three signposts: 'HALT - be SURE - before you use FLAC'.

Often parents say to me, 'If only kids came with an instruction manual.' Each situation with each child is so unique that an Instruction Manual would need to be entitled 'The Never Ending Story'. Like buying a car, the manual can help you discover all the capabilities of the vehicle but you're the one who has to navigate the terrain. There isn't going to be a solution provided for every situation but, with the signposts in this book, you can discover how to create family life that runs more smoothly. And how to be the parent you'd love to be.

There is a chapter for each of the three signposts on how to better connect with your child. We'll also explore how each signpost relates to you as parent. Then you'll find a bridge chapter, to discover why each signpost matters. By the end of this book you will have three easy-to-remember signposts to point you in a helpful direction on your parenting journey. Signposts to give clarity in those crisis moments when you need it the most, but also to remind you that it's the small everyday interactions that build the harmonious home you really want. To avoid the clumsiness of 'she/he' and 'his/her', I use either masculine or feminine in different parts of the book.

You may also notice, I don't tell you what you 'should' do - I prefer to suggest what you 'could' do (in other words, I respect you have a choice).

The incidents and persons in this book are fictitious - and in some ways the story is about all of us on the parenting journey. My two sons are now well into their thirties and I'm grateful they have both turned out fine. I was a qualified and experienced teacher - but it would have saved us all heartache and frustration if I'd known then what I know now. I invite you to discover the secrets of 'BEHAVE - What To Do When Your Child Won't' because I'd love for you to have a calmer, smoother, less circuitous parenting trip than I did.

'I don't care whether you're driving a hybrid or an SUV. If you're heading for a cliff you've got to change direction.' Barack Obama[1]

---

1 HTTP://WWW.BRAINYQUOTE.COM/QUOTES/KEYWORDS/DRIVING.HTML 10/02/2014

CHAPTER ONE

HALT - what's going on for your child?

HALT - what's going on for your child?

♡

Trish stared at the dark ceiling, trying to ignore Derek's deep-throated snores. She sighed to herself. She needed to talk with him about how they were dealing with the kids, but it always seemed to end in a tiff. It wasn't supposed to be like this. They'd waited several years before starting a family and then it was a joint decision. They both wanted kids. Of course they loved them - but nobody told them how damned hard it would be sometimes. Especially Alice. Right from the start she'd been a niggly baby – not like her older sister. Now she was nearly five years old and about to start school. If only they could get her to behave.

Trish's mind wouldn't switch off, as much as she needed to sleep. Derek rolled over and nudged her hand, to stop her tapping her fingers against the bedding. Those annoying red numbers on the clock - 2:05. She eased herself out from under the duvet, trying not to disturb Derek. She slipped on her dressing gown, and headed for the kitchen. Perhaps a cup of chamomile tea would help her to settle.

She opened her iPad to glance at Facebook whilst she waited for the kettle to boil. She smiled at the cute kitten on Sarah's post and hit 'Like'. She swiped the page, glancing over entries when a comment from her friend Louise caught her eye.

A Parenting course?

Why would Louise have done a parenting course? She was so calm and steady with her kids.

A Parenting course? And what was a 'Coaching Approach to Parenting'? Trish clicked the link. Would this give her the answers she was looking for?

Two evenings later Trish found herself and her friend Pam in a semicircle of people much like her. Regular parents doing the regular parenting thing. They spent time identifying what they wanted to cover in the course and now Joy, the facilitator, shared her story.

♡

Being a qualified teacher I thought I knew how to raise children. While I cruised through their early years, by the time my second son was a teenager, family life was sliding out of control.

Somehow I was on a collision course with my second son. He wasn't a 'bad kid' - but I was so determined to be a 'good mother' that our relationship was being eroded. What I wish I'd known when my kids were young was how to reflect on how I was parenting. My mindset was, 'If I could only manage his behaviour!' But it's a fallacy that you can control anyone's behaviour. Parenting workshops are sometimes advertised: *'Managing Children's Behaviour'*. The bottomline is - you can't! It's not possible to manage anyone else's behaviour. Not even your child's. The only person's behaviour you can ever manage is your own. It's impossible to make another person behave the way you want them to. Have you ever tried to get a toddler to eat when he doesn't want to? His cheeks start filling, like hamster cheeks, no matter how much you coo or fly aeroplanes into his mouth. Then brrrp - out it all comes. You can't even manage a toddler's behaviour!

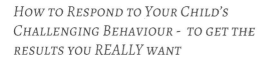

How to Respond to Your Child's Challenging Behaviour - to get the results you REALLY want

So if you can't manage a child's behaviour, what can you do?

You can't make your child behave, but you can create an environment which will encourage cooperative behaviour. Here's how.

Are you sometimes daunted when your child is difficult, unreasonable or uncooperative? Whether it's backchatting, wails of 'You don't love me', angry 'I hate you' darts, homework issues, worries about bullying or self esteem, or one of the other myriad challenges that can wreck your head as a parent - here's the first signpost I wish I'd known - HALT. Perhaps you've come across HALT before? Stay with me because I'll share some unique angles that might give you helpful insights into your child's challenging behaviour.

Regardless of age, when your child starts acting out, use HALT to stop and ask yourself:

H - IS HE HUNGRY?

A – IS HE ANGRY OR ANXIOUS?

L – IS HE LONELY OR ILL?

T - IS HE TIRED?

Let's look at each letter of the 'HALT signpost.

H - IS HE HUNGRY?

This might be physical hunger.

Children will act out when they are hungry.

When asking yourself, 'Is he hungry?' also think, 'Is he thirsty?' Sometimes your child can confuse thirst signals for hunger signals, when what his body needs is fluid. Encourage your child to drink water. Out of control or irritable behaviour can also be triggered by food additives, colourants or extra sugar.[2] Food allergies can also cause upsets.

♡

Joy, the facilitator, was discussing the 'H for Hungry?' when Pam, who was sitting next to Trish, shifted in her seat. 'Can I share what happened with my four year old? About a month ago Peter went to a friend's birthday party. When I fetched him he ran straight onto the road, in front of a car. I couldn't believe it. He didn't stop when I shouted to him and then 'wham'. Thank God he wasn't seriously injured. But a couple of weeks later, after another birthday party, again he wouldn't stop when I told him to. This time I grabbed his arm and kept hold till I had him strapped into his car seat. Now I'm connecting the dots. I guess the sugar overload from all the party goodies upset his system so that he was not able to control himself. If I'd known about 'HALT' I would have made sense of his behaviour instead of scolding him for something he couldn't regulate.'

'Exactly,' nodded Joy, 'When you're faced with out-of-control behaviour, consider whether there is anything in his diet that needs change.'

♡

2 SUNDERLAND 2006: 114

Your child's behaviour might indicate he is hungry for food but also ask yourself whether he might be hungry for attention or hungry for love. Sometimes parents say,

'Oh, he's doing that for attention.'

Yes, possibly he is. But if a child is acting out because he's physically hungry, you give him food. Why would you deprive a child if he's emotionally hungry? Often when I work with parents who are concerned about their child's behaviour, we soon recognise the child has faced some major upheaval in his life. Children will tell you in their behaviour what sometimes they can't tell you in words. If you focus only on how to 'correct' the challenging behaviour, without reflecting on what might lie beneath it, you might be missing your child's 'SOS'. Your child's behaviour might be telling you he is not in an 'okay' place.

The soft-spoken woman on the other side of the room suddenly said, 'My two year old has become aggressive towards me. Her Dad and I were having a hard time and he moved out a couple of weeks ago. Gemma hasn't seen him since. I thought she was too young to understand.'

Joy nodded.

'It makes sense that when a child is 'hungry' for a loved one, she will act out. Thanks for sharing because it illustrates what we're discussing. If you focus only on trying to 'stop the behaviour' you might miss a key opportunity to connect with your child, when your child most needs your reassurance and connection.'

♡

Also consider, 'Is he hungry for play?'

Children have a strong drive to play[3] and if they have not had enough opportunity to work off their natural energy, they will let that energy out any way they can. This is a key one to consider when you are dealing with homework issues. Children have been sitting in school, having to hold in their hunger for play. It makes sense they need to expel this energy before they can settle to a task.

---

3 SUNDERLAND 2006: 104

♡

Martin laughed. He seemed good-natured.

'My three year old Jennifer was always jumping on the furniture. I kept trying to control her behaviour, and stop her jumping but she seemed to be like Tigger, with unstoppable bounce. But then her nursery school teacher told me young children have a such a strong physical need for play - it's a drive they can't resist. So I decided to give her a healthy outlet for her energy.

I bought a trampoline. It's given her a safe space to work off that energy whenever she's staying with me, and she can now respect the limit I've set, "Chairs are for sitting on."

♡

It's more helpful to figure out how to create safe play opportunities for your child than to try to eliminate playful behaviour. Children need to play and work off physical energy. Until a child's hunger is satisfied, whether it's physical hunger or emotional hunger, or play hunger, he will try to get his needs met. When you stop and think about it, this is healthy behaviour! How else would you know his needs - whether they are physical, emotional or play needs?

Play is Nature's way of preparing young creatures, including children, for adult life. Baby seals swim and dive, lion cubs stalk and pounce. The skills learnt in play are essential for living a grown-up life successfully. Your child's play helps him learn physical skills but also helps him to discover how we coperate and work together in community. But it makes sense that sometimes you feel annoyed when your child's fooling around when you have a busy agenda; or you have to deal with his frustrated behaviour when his need to play isn't met. Your stressed reaction will probably melt when you recognise your child's behaviour as a message. And your child is far more likely to cooperate when his physical and emotional needs are met. So first ask yourself, 'Is he hungry?'

A - Is he angry or anxious?

Your child needs emotional support to learn to deal with strong emotions. She is likely to act out when angry or anxious feelings overwhelm her. The key to dealing with aggressive behaviour is to recognise and acknowledge the anger behind it. Anger is always a signal something needs to change.

Angry and anxious feelings will dissolve when your child feels listened to and acknowledged. Instead of scolding your child about how he should behave, you will find your child more cooperative when you respond to what he is experiencing.

♡

Some parents in the group looked puzzled when Joy shared this.
'Let me give you an example,' she said.
'I was visiting my friend who was home from the maternity hospital. Everyone was making a fuss of her and the baby. The doorbell rang and the four year old ran to open the door. As she got to the door, her twelve-year-old brother opened it to let the visitor in. The child went into meltdown, bursting into wails and floods of tears. She wanted to open the door. I figured I needed to do something.
I gave a nod to the visitor to hold on for one minute and I closed the door again.
Then I said, "Oh, you want to let the visitors in. You open the door."
She immediately recovered from her meltdown and opened the door. The visitor went into the room to see the mother and baby, and I knelt, took the child gently by the shoulders, and said, "You can use words to let us know what you need."
'But isn't she getting away with bratty behaviour!' exclaimed Martin. Joy reflected that there had been significant change in the home. It makes sense a young child will need support when she's overwhelmed. By responding to what the four year old needed, rather than trying to CONTROL her behaviour, Joy helped to regain her sense of being of value and to feel competent in the situation. When we connect and communicate our children are more likely to cooperate.

♡

The 'A' in HALT is also a reminder to ask yourself, 'Is she anxious?' Your child might become clingy, bossy or demanding at times when she's feeling anxious. Different children react differently. It's easy to focus on trying to stop your child's behaviour but if you attend to the anxious feelings, the irritating behaviour is more likely to abate. Like other strong emotions, anxiety needs to be heard. The more you learn to listen to your child the more you will know what's needed.

♡

A tired looking lady joined the discussion.
'Our daughter Samantha comes home from school and gorges herself on cake. I'm always giving out to her about putting on weight but that make matters worse. Now that I hear you say: "Is she anxious?", I'm wondering whether she's comfort eating. Perhaps instead of focusing on my child's weight, I need to think about what's going on for her.'

♡

L - Is she lonely or ill?

As a parent, part of your role is to help your child develop the skills to create the friendships she needs to thrive, as well as to learn to be comfortable with her own company.

'If you don't accept yourself fully, you won't live fully, and if you don't live fully you'll need some other way to get full.'   Victoria Moran

♡

'So if Samantha's eating cake because she's anxious, what might that anxiety be telling you?' asked Joy.
'I think she's lonely. She doesn't have friends at school,' replied Samantha's mother.
'So what's needed?' asked Joy.
The discussion unfolded. Samantha needed a strategy to develop friendships. Her parents needed to focus on the longer-term challenge of supporting their child to develop stronger self-esteem and social skills to

handle the school situation.
'HALT matters whatever age your child,' Trish realised. Samantha's
mother relaxed into the chair, nodding. Obviously it had registered
with her that 'Lonely?' was the issue troubling her daughter.

♡

It's important to recognise the difference between being lonely and being alone. Some children are content in their own company. Or they can feel lonely even when they're in a crowd. When we're lonely we feel isolated and dejected even if there are people all around. But we can be alone and feel fine. We can feel 'all one' - complete in ourselves.

The 'L' of HALT is also a reminder to check whether your child is becoming iLL. Often children sickening with something start acting out because they aren't feeling 100% and may need care and special attention. At the same time, it's important not to be putting ideas of illness into your child's head. When you say,
'Have you got a sore tummy?' your child will agree with your diagnosis! Rather, ask her to tell you about how she is feeling. Sore tummies or headaches can be symptoms of anxiety. A listening ear may be a better remedy than a tablet. The more you connect and communicate with your child, the more you will be in tune with what is needed.
Emotional upsets often manifest as body discomfort. If you speed in with the 'spoonful of something', you may be creating a life-long pattern of dependency on medication, instead of helping your child to learn to listen to what her body is telling her. (And of course this is equally important for boys). The 'spoonful of something' may appear to be the quick fix if you have a busy agenda, but what do you model when you reach for pills at the slightest complaint?

A spoonful of medicine isn't going to take away the issue concerning your child. If you become aware of a pattern, find the space to connect and ask,
 'I notice you have a sore tummy on Monday mornings.
What might this sore tummy be telling us?'
Your response can help your child to learn to choose healthy options. You can develop your child's personal awareness and her ability to communicate about things which trouble her. Help her to learn to

articulate what she needs.

And of course there are times when crankiness can be a sign of illness. You, as parent, contuitively know your child. What I mean by 'contuitively' is the blend of your conscious knowledge and your intuition. When you take the time and space to consciously hear her and to intuitively tune in with your heart as well as your head, you will contuitively know what response is needed.

T - 'IS SHE RUNNING A TEMPERATURE?' OR 'TIRED?'

If your child is running a temperature, her behaviour may be difficult; but behavioural issues can also arise if she's too hot or too cold. Young children don't always recognise they are over-hot and need to be reminded to take off their extra clothing.

Sometimes you may overlook the obvious with an 'out of sorts' child. Overtired children, who don't get enough sleep on a regular basis, can be difficult. A regular routine where your child is settled in bed is key to getting enough sleep.

Your child may resist having a set bedtime, but over-late nights and crankiness are often bed-partners. If 'Tired' seems to be the issue, dealing with the long-term cause is going to get better results than dealing with the symptom. The cranky behaviour may be a signal to establish a more consistent bedtime routine.

'Tired' also refers to children being tired of sitting still too long - in a restaurant, in school or doing homework. Or tired of being shut in the house all day. As Martin observed, children have a 'hunger for play' - when they respond to their play drive they are not being naughty. They are doing what children are intended to do. Letting you know they need to play. The challenge is to balance your adult agenda with the needs of your child.

♡

Trish was looking forward to the next Parenting session. She was excited to share her experience.

'The car trip after school is a nightmare. Often Alice starts it, but the kids niggle and squabble all the way home. The twenty minute drive wrecks my head and I'm frazzled and shouting by the time we pull into our driveway. But after learning the HALT signpost last week I figured they were probably hungry. So each morning this week I've prepared a snack-box for each child for the trip home.

And I've even done the healthy bit - they're munching fruit and nuts. It's worked. The fighting on the way home from school has reduced by about eighty per cent!'

♡

TO SUM UP

When you react to your child's challenging behaviour, without stopping to think, it's like braking on an oil slick. Things easily slide out of control. When you HALT and reflect on what might be behind your child's behaviour, you will find a helpful way forward.

So here's a quick overview of 'HALT'.

H Is he hungry? Or thirsty?
  Is he hungry for play?
  Or for attention?
A Is he angry or anxious?
L Is he lonely or ill?
T is he tired?

Sometimes it's hard to be the parent you want to be, even when you have the best of intentions. So, in the next chapter we'll look at HALT - regarding yourself as Parent, and why this matters if you want a calmer, happier home.

CHAPTER TWO

HALT - what do you need?
Why Your Self Care Matters

HALT - what do you need?
Why Your Self Care Matters

♡

Trish clinked the spoon against the side of her latte glass. It was good to have time to relax with Louise while the little ones were with her mother. She remembered the group contract requested confidentiality - everyone's personal stories were to remain in the room. 'But do feel free to tell your friends and family about the principles you learn,' said Joy. Trish and Louise had been friends since their first year at school. She always felt safe to share with Louise.

'I went home so excited after the Parenting evening. HALT made so much sense to me when I thought about Alice's behaviour, but I'm finding it so hard to be the parent I want to be, even though I can see how her behaviour makes sense.'

Louise nibbled her cinnamon cookie.

'It sometimes seems to me, learning more about what children need to thrive makes Parenting harder, not easier. But it's worth it. I'm so much more aware of thinking about my child's perspective now. When I'm battling to be the parent I want to be I find it helps to apply HALT to myself as well as to my child.'

'How do you mean?' asked Trish.

♡

The kids are driving you mad. They are whining, acting out, at each other's throats or giving you a hard time.

This may be the time to HALT and consider how it applies to you, as parent, as well. When your child gets under your skin it may be because for too long you haven't stopped to address your own needs.

None of us can keep on giving to others if our own basic needs aren't met.

Think of the airline safety instructions you hear as you're waiting for take-off,

'Put on your own oxygen mask before you help your child.'
You're not able to meet your child's needs if you haven't looked after your own. So look again at HALT from your own perspective.

H - Are you Hungry?

Perhaps you need something to eat or drink.

♡

Trish laughed when Lousie said this.
'Yeah, a vodka would help!'
Louise smiled. 'There are times when that is tempting. You know one of the scariest things I've ever experienced was with a woman who was horribly drunk. Her toddler kept trying to get her attention but it was like - "the lights are on but nobody's home." He'd look and look into her eyes and say, "Mummy, Mummy," but he couldn't connect with her. I'll never forget the sad puzzlement in his little face. I'd never realised before how much having one too many can cut me off from being there for my kids, at a practical level and emotionally too. Seriously though, if you're thirsty or hungry, particularly if your sugar levels drop, it's easy to react to the kids.'

♡

Hungry for some adult company?

Perhaps you're hungry for attention? It's easy to expect somebody else 'should' give that to you - but do you give attention to yourself?
Maybe you are hungry for self care? Give some attention to yourself! You will be surprised how much easier you deal with the challenges of parenting when your own tank is full. Discover for yourself what 'fills your tank' by noticing the activities that leave you feeling joyful and fulfilled afterwards. It's different things for different people but most of us need time with good friends, time in Nature or asethetically pleasing environments, time for sporting or creative activities. If your emotional tank is empty you can't be the parent you want to be.

♡

Louise sighed and smiled at Trish, 'You think I've got it altogether as a parent. I learnt the hard way. I was so focused on being a "good" mother and wife, I wasn't minding myself. When a close friend, a psychologist, expressed her concern for me, I told her I didn't have time to look after my own needs - that would come later. But less than a year later, I found myself in crisis.'

Trish couldn't believe what she was hearing. She reached over the table and put her hand on Louise's. How come she'd never heard this! Then she figured this was whilst she and Derek were off 'seeing the world' before they settled to have kids.

'I'm sorry, Louise, I never realised,' she whispered.

'That's okay,' smiled Louise. 'I never told you. I was so depressed I couldn't talk to anyone and my self-esteem had fallen through the floorboards. I'd become such a ragbag that our marriage was nearly on the rocks. I was worried we'd end up separating.

I guess I could have blamed Rod that he wasn't minding me - but fortunately I recognised the only person who was responsible for my happiness was me. It took us a while to turn things round. I mean, it took us time to get in this situation so it needed time to get back on track. It wasn't always easy.'

Trish smiled. It was obvious Louise and her husband were in a good place together now.

'You know,' Louise continued. 'In Japanese the word for crisis also means "opportunity". I couldn't see it then but our relationship challenge proved to be an incredible opportunity for personal growth. Sometimes I wonder how much pain, for all concerned, might have been avoided if I'd taken time to seriously HALT and figure out what was needed when my friend shared her concern for my well-being. What I do know is it's possible to turn things around and create the relationship you want - but it starts with yourself.'

♡

A - Are you Angry or Anxious?

How are you feeling?

When you are angry or frustrated, ask yourself, 'What's the change I need?' Often as a parent, you give so much attention to your children you forget you have needs too. You can't give to your child if your emotional fuel tank is empty. When you are anxious, take time to figure out what is going on for you and what you need to do about it.

It's easy to think, 'My child doesn't respect me.' But do you respect yourself? You might be thinking, 'I need my family to appreciate me.' But do you appreciate yourself? Don't ask from anyone else what you're not already giving to yourself.

Of course there may be a genuine cause for your anxiety or anger. [4]

If so, what are the practical steps you need to take?

If your anxiety is a gnawing grey fog, where you can't identify what is the issue, it's probably saying something about your needs.

Where do you find support to understand what's going on for you and your child? To bring clarity to the situation?

♡

In the next Parenting session, Trish shared her awareness about applying HALT to herself.

Joy nodded. 'What do you need to do to mind yourself; to keep yourself in 'good running order?'

Martin joined in. 'I'm a taxi driver. My car's been round the clock but she still runs as sweet as a dream. It's not just minding the fuel and tyre pressures. I regularly have her serviced. She wouldn't be reliable if I didn't give her the attention she needs. I guess we're in parenting for the long-haul – so we need to ask ourselves what's the "regular maintenance programme" we need.'

'Yes,' said Trish. 'It makes sense we need to give ourselves the same outer and inner attention.'

Joy smiled. 'And sometimes we may need the major overhaul. But ask yourself what would be even a ten minute top-up to put "fuel in your tank" today.'

---

4 THERE WILL BE MORE ON DEALING WITH ANGRY OR ANXIOUS THOUGHTS IN THE SEQUEL TO THIS BOOK: 'LISTEN - WHAT TO DO WHEN YOUR CHILD WON'T'

29

♡

Notice what activities leave you feeling recharged and re-energised and then figure out how to build these into your life.

L - Are you Lonely or ill?

Perhaps you're feeling lonely. You might be so caught up with your child's activities you've lost contact with your own friends and colleagues. We all need the stimulation of adult company.
When did you last have quality time:
With good friends?
With your spouse or partner?
Or perhaps you're feeling lonely because you've lost contact with yourself. When did you last have quality time with yourself - whether taking a walk, doing a creative activity, journalling or meditating?

♡

As the group discussed this Pam laughed,
'I love Oprah's expression - she doesn't have lunch "by herself" but "with herself".'
Trish was still thinking about having time 'with herself' as she leaned over the bed to kiss Alice's plump little cheek. Mmmm - that fresh child smell. She stroked a stray strand of her sleeping child's red hair, which lay on her forehead. Her heart filled with such love it leaked through her eyes. Alice was so peaceful when she was asleep - if only she was always so angelic!
Trish thought how hard it was for her to HALT and notice what Alice's challenging behaviour might be trying to say when there were other people around, particularly her mother-in-law. That arched eyebrow when Alice misbehaved was the last thing Trish needed! 'I guess if I'm not feeling okay about myself I'll find it hard to be the parent Alice needs me to be.' She remembered Joy's words:
'If you don't have a sense of being complete in yourself you'll be expecting someone else, perhaps your child or spouse, to fill the "hole in your soul".'
Before she went to bed, Trish took out her new journal and spent a few

lines penning where she needed to HALT and give attention to herself.
It would all start with how she was!

♡

At times you may need to HALT to check whether you're feeling ill.
If you're ill, feeling unwell, what are you doing about it? Sometimes recognising you're not feeling 100% can help you to figure it's you feeling cranky that's the issue, more than your child's behaviour. Or perhaps your crankiness might help you recognise something is not okay in your own life and needs to be dealt with.

You won't get the connection your children need unless you connect with yourself, so keep in tune with your body. If you're feeling unwell or stressed, what message is your body giving you? And when you're uptight, unless your child's behaviour is putting someone at risk, it will probably be more helpful to leave dealing with it till another day when you feel more able to handle it.

As a parent you often focus on the issue which needs to be solved. And it's amazing, when you HALT and are in a comfortable place in yourself, you connect and communicate, then most of the issues naturally resolve.

T - Are you Tired?

Throughout history, for thousands of years, parenting has been part of the wider context of family and community. Now the responsibility often rests on the shoulders of only one or two parents. No wonder you feel exhausted, irritable and worn out sometimes. If there are things going on in your own life which are tough to handle - get the support you need!

♡

Maeve had hardly spoken in the group since she'd shared about her husband leaving home. But now she interrupted:

'Support's fine in theory. But I'm a single mum! I've got to be up in the morning for work, even if I've had a sleepless night. There's nobody to share the load, no matter how bad I'm feeling.'

Joy nodded. 'It makes sense that you're feeling overloaded. And at least you're taking time to be here and enjoy our support.

Think of it this way: A small hut needs little foundation to hold it steady. But a large apartment building needs a substantial foundation. In the same way, the bigger the challenges you face, the more substantial support you need.

When my kids were young and I felt wobbly I'd often grumble at myself that I should be strong! It would have been more helpful to recognise, "This is a big challenge I'm facing. How do I get the help I need?"

The going is tough for you right now because you're in a relationship crisis and you still have your daily responsibilites to deal with. Who are the people who support you? Who are the people in your life whose presence encourages you, so you feel a sense of hope you can come through this? Who gives you the confidence you can deal with the challenges?'

♡

When you recognise the people who give you the genuine support you need, you can choose the company that energises and encourages you. And of course, there's the practical help too, whether it's the friend or family member who child-minds for the evening or offers to collect some groceries for you when you're under stress. When you have the support you need and you are in an okay space in yourself, it's easier to look objectively at your children's behaviour, without becoming entangled in it.

♡

The kids were settled in bed - early for once. Derek was in the study, figuring the month end finances. Trish snatched a few moments to phone Louise. It was a while since they'd chatted.

'How's the course going?' Louise asked.

'Great - but challenging. Being more aware makes a difference some of the time.' sighed Trish. 'But Alice pushes my buttons in a way the other two never do. I wake in the morning and think,
"Right, I'll remember HALT - we'll have a good day today." And before we've even got breakfast over she and I are fighting about something. I can't handle her.'
Louise laughed. 'You've got your third session tonight? Wait and see what you discover.'

♡

TO SUM UP

When relationships are challenging HALT and ask yourself these questions:
AM I HUNGRY ?
ANGRY? ANXIOUS?
LONELY? OR ILL?
AM I TIRED OR DO I HAVE A TEMPERATURE?
Your answers give you the insight to shift things in a more helpful direction. When your needs are met, you will be more aware of what's needed to create a more enjoyable and fulfilling family life.

In the next chapter you'll discover a key tool for creating the change you want - 'react or respond'.

♡

Trish started the morning optimistic and looking forward to the Parenting course that evening. But Alice played up from the moment she woke. She wouldn't get dressed without Trish helping her. She picked at her jam on toast, even though she had chosen it. Trish tried to remain pleasant but she could feel her patience oozing out her shoes. It was time for Derek to drop the children to school and Alice didn't even have her coat

CHAPTER THREE

React or Respond - it's your choice

on. React or Respond - it's your choice

Trish glared at Alice, her throat tightening. 'ALICE - get your coat on now!'

Alice glared back with that defiant look in her eyes. Trish felt like shaking her.

'Did you hear me? I'm not talking again!'

Stubborn silence. Was this the little angel who looked so cute asleep?

'Alice! NOW!'

Derek stepped in.

'Ok. Trish.' He knelt. 'Do you want Daddy to put your coat on for you?'

Alice's big baby eyes gazed up at him in all sweetness and she held her arms out.

Trish stormed out the room and started clanging the dishes in the sink. How did this little mite have such control over her! And she had her father twisted round her little finger.

Derek called out they were ready to go. Trish took a big breath and went into the hallway. She kissed Jamie goodbye and then tried to kiss Alice. But she turned her cheek away and nestled into her father.

Oooh, she was so stubborn!

Trish would have some questions for Joy tonight!

♡

In the session, Joy discussed how she used to often notice how much easier it was to be patient with the children she taught, than with her own children. When we're emotionally invested, it's much harder to be objective. Parenting is the most important job you'll ever do and because of your deep connection with your child, it isn't always easy to remain clear-headed and reasonable. It makes sense you sometimes get stressed about your child's behaviour. You are anxious about your child's safety and well-being, and if you are anything like I was, you are also concerned, 'What will other people think!'

'The people who mind don't matter, and the people who matter don't mind.'
Dr Suess[5]

---

5 HTTP://WWW.QUOTATIONSPAGE.COM/QUOTES/DR._SEUSS 01/11/2014

Whether you're dealing with sibling rivalry, a whining child, answering you back, eating challenges, homework issues, stealing or any other challenging behaviour, - as much as you want your child to change, the only person you can change is yourself. That's good news, because you can change yourself.

A small cog can be vital to drive huge machinery and it's often small changes which makes the difference to keep home life running smoothly. *React or Respond* is the key to create the change you need.

REACT
- when your reptilian brain seizes control

Whether world war three has broken out in your home or it's somewhere you're all glad to live can depend on whether you, as parent, choose to react or to respond.

We often use these two words, react or respond, as though they mean the same thing but let's rethink this. What's the difference between

react and respond? Remember, when you were a child, finding that spot where you tap the knee and your leg swings out. A 'knee-jerk reaction' happens automatically, whereas a response is when you examine the causes or facts, before taking action. To better understand the difference between reacting and responding, let's look at neuroscience. Just as a mechanic keeps the motor running sweetly because he knows what's under the bonnet, knowing how the brain works is strategic in your parenting. In the last ten years neuroscientists have discovered more about how the human brain works than in the whole of human history. If you know how the human brain works and what it needs to thrive, you will know how to respond, rather than react, to your child's challenging behaviour.

We tend to say 'the human brain' as though we have only one brain. But neuroscientists tell us we have three parts of our brain; each so distinct in a sense we have three brains.
The outer layer of the brain is the cortex - this is the thinking part of the brain.
Deeper within is the limbic system - the part of the brain which does most of the emotional work.

The innermost part of the brain is often called the 'reptilian brain'. This part of the brain deals with survival instincts. Whether it's the kids fighting or the house on fire, this part of the brain rings the alarm bells when something is not okay. Now if there's a fire, or someone might get hurt, this reptilian part of the brain is vital for getting out of danger. This is the part of the brain wired for survival. It triggers an immediate fight, flight or freeze reaction. This instant call to action can make the split-second difference between life and death.
Think of times when you instinctively swing the car out of harm's way, or when you grab the toddler who's about to put something in an electric socket. In these situations you don't think through your choices - you instantly react to avoid harm.

The reptilian part of the brain is great for survival but it can't tell the difference between genuine danger and your raging child. If that part of the brain registers 'emergency' you will react, even at times when this won't be helpful, unless you're aware. Just as crocodiles don't do much caring and connecting, your reptilian brain isn't into developing caring relationships. The reptilian brain reacts to survive. Its job is survival. In family interactions you want to do more than survive. Everyone needs connection. Your child needs you to model engaging human interaction skills, which happens when you make a 'whole brain' response.

It takes a combination of this inner reptilian brain, your limbic system, which is the 'emotions' part of your brain, and your reasoning outer brain, called the cortex, to respond in a 'whole brain' mature way, especially in challenging situations.[6] When you are calm and in touch with yourself and your situation, all three parts of the brain interact, without you even noticing. But when something signals danger, your reptilian brain becomes wide-awake and goes into over-drive. At times when you want to connect rather than merely survive, you need to calm your reptilian brain.

RESPOND
- How to Calm Your Reptilian Brain

When something upsetting happens the reptilian part of the brain is triggered. It takes the outer thinking part of your brain a few milliseconds to catch up. Counting to ten (preferably in Roman numerals) can avoid an unhelpful reaction. It gives the thinking part of the brain time to reconnect. If you want to respond rather than react, take a few breaths to calm yourself.

Practise breathing in to the count of seven 1-2-3-4-5-6-7 and out to eleven: 8 - 9 -10 -11.

Be aware of where you are. Use all your senses to bring you into the

6 SIEGEL AND HARTZELL 2006: 73,74

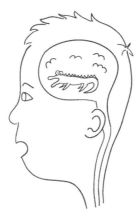

present moment. Notice what you can see around you, feel, hear, taste or smell right now.

Ground yourself. Become present to your surroundings and the people with you rather than chasing the reactive thoughts in your head. Then you will become calmer and the thinking part of your brain will re-engage. Focus on creating connection. Keep HALT in mind - recognise if you or your child is:

Hungry,

Angry, Anxious,

Lonely, iLL

or

Tired.

Ask yourself, 'What's really needed here?'

HALT. Choose to respond rather than react. Recognise if your child needs attention. By HALTing to reflect what might be going on for yourself and for your child, you will can create a helpful response, rather than lashing out with a crocodilian survival reaction.

Taming Your Wild Thoughts

A key factor in *reacting* or *responding* is the thoughts you tell yourself. When you feed yourself stories,

'He's trying to annoy me.'

'This will never end.'

'I can't cope' - you are feeding your crocodile brain. You are causing a survival 'fight or flight' reaction, rather than a helpful response which creates connection.

So how do you get rid of negative thoughts? You'd like to negate them but it's not that simple. They have a nasty habit of reappearing when you try to eliminate them. But you can replace them with more helpful thoughts. Remind yourself your child's behaviour is about him - your reponse is about you. Think about being the parent you want to be. Imagine the positive outcome you want. Focus your thoughts on what is within your control - and what's in your control is how you choose to be.

What's Happening in the Brain - REACT or RESPOND?

When you allow negative thoughts to overwhelm you, your brain releases stress chemicals and this causes 'emotional flooding'. This means your brain's energy concentrates in the reptilian part of your brain. It's on red alert. And the outer cortex, the thinking part of the brain, is temporarily 'out of commission'.

One way I imagine this is as though the brain is an international newspaper headquarters. There's a busy chief-editor in charge:

'Put that on the front page. Bin that. Coffee please. That to the sports section.'
And the instructions are carried out. But if there were a sudden flood in the building, and the editor's room flooded, all helpful communication in or out would be suspended. When you are emotionally flooded, meaningful communication, either coming in or going out, becomes impossible.

To have the chief-editor in charge, you need your outer cortex engaged, so you can figure out what's needed and make effective decisions. When you talk calmly, positively and reassuringly to yourself, you calm the reptilian part of your brain. You reconnect with your ability to be reason-able (able to reason!) and to appreciate your child's perspective. You need the cortex - the 'thinking' part of the brain to be engaged to do this. Then you can connect with your child's experience. You can choose to make a whole brain response rather than react.

♡

Trish listened in fascination as Joy explained about the three sections of the brain.
'My crocodile brain was alive and well this morning,' she exclaimed.
She shared about how she and Alice got into a power struggle that

morning.

'Derek had two four year olds to deal with, I was so wound up,' she said. 'I'm thinking, if Alice was having a bad day, her crocodile must have been snapping away - and what she needed was for me to stay calm. From now on I'm going to consciously choose to respond. It's me as parent who's responsible to create calm.'

Joy smiled. 'Yes. As parent, you're responsible. You're response - able. Able to respond - when your chief-editor is in charge. The emotional temperature in the home is your responsibility. If you're a thermometer, you allow yourself to react; the emotional heat rises uncontrollably. Rather choose to be an 'emotional thermostat' in your home. You are the one responsible for the 'emotional climate control'.

Trish sighed. 'I wish I'd known about this before I got out of bed this morning.'

Martin grinned. 'Don't worry. I'm sure Alice will give you plenty more opportunities!'

♡

Four Practical Tips - Making it Easier to 'Respond'

Soon you'll discover how to hold a limit when you have stressful situations like Trish described. In the meantime here are some practical

tips on how to remain in respond mode at times when your 'crocodile' starts snapping.

Tip 1:
Use gerunds to remind children of the behaviour you expect.
Gerunds are short phrases, said in a firm, friendly tone. When you repeat it often, it reminds your child of the behaviour you expect. For example, when you eat out at a restaurant you might say 'sitting nicely' or 'good table manners'. It's a short, specific, gentle phrase which reminds your child of what you have discussed at other times about the behaviour you expect. So rather than a stream of negative instructions: 'Pull your chair in to the table. Eat your food over your plate. Take little bites and empty your mouth before putting more in your mouth. Don't kick the chair,' instead say, 'Sitting nicely.' A gerund is a brief, friendly reminder to your child of the behaviour you expect.

Tip 2:
Word instructions in the positive.
When you say, 'Don't run' your child hears 'Run', so rather turn the statement around into a positive statement of what you do want.

For instance, instead of saying, 'Don't run,' say, 'Walk.'

Likewise if your child is standing in front of the television when you're trying to watch it, rather than saying, 'Don't stand in front of the TV,' say something like,

'You can come and sit next to me and watch TV or you can play on the other side of the room.'

Tip 3:

If your child is busy, give a few minutes warning when it's time to end that activity.

This is important if your child is engaged in what he's doing.

Say, for instance, the children are rough and tumbling with dad.

Everyone is bouncing around madly and now it's time to stop. Like slowing a car, you don't go straight from fifth gear to first. Slide down through the gears. Gradually ease the level of the play. Warn them play will stop in a few minutes. Encourage less energetic movement, like arranging the pillows on the bed - and gradually ease them into 'second gear' and then into 'first'.

A gradual shift down in the energy of the play can help move through a transition in a pleasant and cooperative way.

Tip 4:

Give clear instructions, use a firm, clear tone of voice and eye contact to show you mean it.

I remember watching a father rough-and-tumbling with his son. It was time to end the play.

'Please stop now,' Dad repeatedly requested whilst his son continued to bash him relentlessly with the pillow. The son was not getting the message that the game was over because Dad wasn't making it clear.

Use a firm, authorative tone of voice, clear body language and eye contact so your child knows what is expected. This is not a time to use 'please'. 'Please' is a request, which may be ignored. You are not making a request, you are setting a limit.

Sometimes your child may ignore your instruction because he doesn't register it. If you yell instructions at your child over your shoulder as you dash out the door they will go unheeded. Rather, move into arm's length, make definite eye contact and address your child calmly and clearly by name, and give the instruction or request.

TO SUM UP

When you're tempted to react, first check in with yourself whether your child has a clear picture of what is expected of him. Use a gerund - a brief, positive phrase that reminds your child what behaviour you expect. Give your child opportunity to 'change gear' and use a friendly-but-firm tone to indicate you mean business.

To react or to respond is your choice. Your child needs you to remain the adult. One person having a meltdown is enough! Calm your reptilian brain by focusing on your breathing and by choosing thoughts which help you be the way you want to be in this situation. Choose a 'whole brain' response if you want a calmer, more cooperative family life.

What 'emotional temperature' is your home: ice-cold, raging hot or pleasantly warm? The choice is yours.

You're probably saying,

 'But if you knew my kids...' so in the next chapter we'll look at how to 'be SURE' when your child's behaviour is challenging.

CHAPTER FOUR

'Be SURE' - what's going on for your child

'be SURE' - what's going on for your child

♡

Trish's fingers drummed on the steering wheel. She sighed at the slow swish, swish of the wipers. Would the traffic lights ever turn green!

Some evenings it was so hard to get out the house.

'I'm going to be late,' she thought.

The kids seemed to always need something just when she was about to leave.

By the time she arrived, the group was already in discussion.

She slipped onto the empty seat next to Martin. Joy gave a quick smile to acknowledge her and kept her focus on Maureen. Trish knew Maureen's two daughters were much the same age as hers, but didn't know much else about her yet.

Trish's brow crinkled and a half smile played on her lips as she listened to Maureen's story. It was easy to identify with this.

'So I walk into the garden and my nine year old, Jane, is having a tiff with her little sister, who's five years younger. I mean, it's not an equal playing field, so I intervene.

"Stop fighting with your sister," I say to Jane. "She's only little."

I decided it best to separate them so I took my little one by the hand and started going into the house.

I don't know why but something made me swing round.

And there was Jane, sticking her tongue out at me.

She got such a shock - she must have imagined I had eyes in the back of my head.

Jane's normally such a good, cooperative child, I don't think she's ever done that before.

But I caught her with her pink tongue protruding out of her cross little face. Before I had a chance to say anything she said, "I was sticking my tongue out at my sister."

I didn't believe her but I guess she was worried she was in big trouble.

I was in such turmoil.

Part of me wanted to give Jane a good smack for her cheeky behaviour.

The other part of me was hurt. When I saw the anger in her little face I thought, "She doesn't love me."

I felt awful. I scolded her and told her not to be naughty. Was there some-

48

thing I could have done?"
Trish nodded in sympathy. Sometimes it's so hard to know how to respond even when you are focused on parenting helpfully.

♡

Have you ever been in a situation where you feel like tearing your hair out with your kids? Or when you've felt hurt by their behaviour? When you most want to react is when your child most needs your response. When you think calmly, instead of reacting, you can figure out what's going on for your child and what is needed.

A useful signpost to guide you in a helpful direction to respond, rather than react, is SURE.

The SURE signpost stands for

S - Separate out her behaviour from her personhood.

U - Understand all behaviour has a cause and all behaviour has an intention.

R - Respond from a place of separate-ness and understanding.

E - Ensure safety.

Let's look at Maureen's story. She was glad she'd kept calm enough not to react when she caught Jane sticking out her tongue at her. She could change a survive moment into a thrive opportunity. Here's how:

S –Separate out her behaviour from her personhood.

Use words to describe how you feel about your child's action, rather than attacking her character. It's more helpful to say, 'I'm not happy you were sticking out your tongue,' than to accuse her of being a 'bad girl'. If you label your child she will feel attacked. Then her crocodile reactivity will start snapping even more strongly than it already is, plunging her into fight or flight mode. Either way it will be impossible for her to see your point of view. Rather than labelling her, comment on the particular behaviour: 'I don't like it when you ... I'd prefer it if you ...'
Because your child may have done something you don't like does not make her a 'bad girl', or a 'bold girl' (as we would say in Ireland). Similarly, doing something you like does not make her a 'good girl'. This is a behaviour, it's not her person.

U - Understand all behaviour has a cause and all behaviour has an intention.

Ask yourself:
'What might this behaviour be telling me?'
'And what else might it be telling me?'
'And what else? '
It makes sense Jane's behaviour was caused by her jealous or overwhelmed feelings. Possibly it was a boundary issue between her and her sister. Jane needed support to deal with these feelings and to learn how to handle conflict. Situations like these create an opportunity to help your child learn to deal with powerful emotions and the challenging relationship situations we face in everyday life.

R - Respond from a place of Separateness and Understanding.

How do you do this?

Remember to focus on your breath - 'In 1-2-3-4-5-6-7; out 8-9-10-11' for a few breaths to let your thinking brain catch up with your reptilian brain. Consciously choose to respond rather than react.

Respond from a place of understanding. Imagine this situation from her perspective. Imagine how she might be feeling and what she might be needing. When you most want to react is when your child most needs your compassionate response.

Trust your contuition (your conscious knowledge combined with your intuition) to create a helpful response. You won't get it 'perfect' every time but your child will sense when you come from a place of caring and connection.

E - Ensure safety.

You need to ensure physical safety and also ensure emotional safety. Your child does not yet understand your behaviour is about you. If you act as though she's bad - she'll believe she's bad. She might think she is unworthy of your love. While emotions are still heated, do something like going for a walk together, so you can calm yourselves. Later, you will both be reason-able again (able to reason because the reptilian brain has calmed and you can now engage in a whole-brain response). Use an 'I' statement about that particular incident: 'I don't like it when you stick out your tongue at me. I'd prefer it if you tell me in words if you're feeling angry or upset.' When you choose to respond rather than react, you address the behaviour, rather than attack your child's character. Your response leaves your child feeling 'okay' about herself.

Also ensure the emotional safety of any onlookers, particularly other children. What I wish I'd known when my kids were young was the impact on everyone concerned, including siblings, when I reacted.

If your child was frightened by a fierce wild animal he would automatically run to you for protection, right? It's easy to react and 'lose the cool' but where does your child go for safety if it's you who's raging?

When you react everyone can be left feeling raw and ragged afterward, (yourself included).

And when there are onlookers, particularly other children, they can be left with painful feelings and memories about an upsetting experience. React or respond. It's your choice. Nobody can drive you crazy without your consent.

Transform survive moments into thrive opportunities.

If you connect with your child's experience you get to understand what's needed. Transform survive moments into thrive opportunities. In a survive moment, like when your child sticks out her tongue at you, she's feeling strong emergency emotions, like fear or anger. You can react and shut down any communication and connection by scolding or punishing the child, or you can acknowledge your child's emotion. When you name your child's feeling, ('You're feeling angry right now.') she can claim it ('Oh, yeah, I am feeling angry!'). When she can claim her emotion she can tame it. (She can control the emotion rather than the emotion controlling her). A thrive moment is created when you provide the space and safety for all your child's feelings to be acknowledged, even the challenging ones, so she can learn how to name, claim and tame them.

♡

'That's all very well,' Martin interjected as Joy discussed this. 'But I want my child to respect other people. To grow up to be polite.'

'Yes,' agreed Joy. 'Your child needs to know certain behaviours aren't okay. But most unsuitable social behaviours disappear once the emotional needs are met and boundaries are established. Your child will absorb the message, "Pulling faces isn't okay" when you discuss it afterwards; once you've connected and you're both calm.'

'But aren't I letting her get away with brattish behaviour?' asked Maureen. Joy smiled. 'When your child is acting out she's already emotionally flooded. The rational part of her brain is disengaged and she's not going to take any meaningful learning from the situation. Like an upset crocodile, she's in fight, flight or freeze mode. Crocodiles don't reason. Crocodiles don't do connection.

What's more helpful is to create the opportunity for you both to move from this reptilian survive mode to whole-brain connection, by responding rather than reacting.'

♡

When you follow the 'be SURE' signpost, you move in a more helpful direction, which will guide you to make sense of your child's challenging behaviour. Learn to recognise when you are being triggered and choose to HALT, and be SURE about what's needed here to recreate emotional safety - both for yourself and for your child.

Remember the road safety instruction we learned as children:

Stop - Look - Listen

It's a good way to be Sure - just add Love.

Stop - Look - Listen - Love.

The more you are aware, the more you'll be able to use a 'whole brain response' rather than a reptilian brain reaction.

When your child regularly experiences your desire to connect, this strengthens his sense of worth, which is one of the three aspects of self-esteem.[7] Your child's self-esteem is probably his most powerful defence against challenging situations in life.

Of course, we're all human and you're not always going to respond as you'd like to. It's easy as a parent to feel guilty about the times when you didn't parent the way you want to. The good news is that when we persist with the change we want it becomes embedded. Neuroscientists now know when positive change happens, our brains develop new healthier links.[8] This can happen at any age. It's never too late to develop new behaviours and attitudes - new brain links - to be the parent you want to be.

And the good news is that when you respond, rather than react, the 'problem' behaviour often naturally disappears because the underlying issue is resolved.[9] There will still be challenges - but they become growth opportunities for both of you.

♡

By the time Trish set off for home the rain had eased. She turned the radio on to Lyrics FM. What she needed - some light classical music. Her brain was saturated from all she'd absorbed in the evening.

'HALT - be SURE.'

'Funny,' she thought. 'I need a licence to drive a car. But there's no requirement at all to parent. I read all the baby books when I was

---

7 JUUL (1995) RE THIS MODEL OF SELF ESTEEM

8 SIEGEL AND HARTZEL, 2004: 33,34

9 FOR MORE ABOUT HOW TO CONNECT WITH YOUR CHILD, WATCH OUT FOR MY NEXT BOOK, 'LISTEN - WHAT TO DO WHEN YOUR CHILD WON'T'.

pregnant but then I believed I had it all sorted. I never realized it's an ongoing learning process if you want your family to thrive.'

♡

TO SUM UP

Here's an overview of SURE:

S —SEPARATE OUT HER BEHAVIOUR FROM HER PERSONHOOD.
This is a one-off reactive behaviour. This does not make her a 'defiant child', 'an aggressive child' or an 'ungrateful child'. Avoid labels! A behaviour incident does not define who your child is as a person.

U - UNDERSTAND.
Understand all behaviour has a cause and all behaviour has an intention. And the intention of the behaviour is usually the need for attention.

R - RESPOND FROM A PLACE OF BEING SEPARATE YET CONNECTED.
And also respond from a place of understanding. Your child's behaviour is about her, your response is about you.

AND E - ENSURE SAFETY.
Ensure the physical and emotional safety of yourself, your child and any onlookers.

In the next chapter we'll look at how to 'be SURE' regarding yourself and why this matters.

CHAPTER FIVE

'be SURE' - regarding yourself

'be SURE' - regarding yourself

As Trish drove home she pictured her mother-in-law's sliding eyebrow. It wasn't that she said anything, it was that expression on her face - Trish knew she was judging her. Disapproving of the way she handled the kids. If Alice even answered her back, let alone stick out her tongue, Derek's mum would be shocked.

'And when I'm judged about the way I parent, whether it's Derek, his mother or even a total stranger in the supermarket, I react. When I'm upset I open my mouth before I've engaged my brain. It's so much harder to respond, to slow down enough to figure what's needed and what really matters!'

She wiped away an angry tear with the back of her hand.

'How can I be the parent I want to be when I'm so wrapped up in what others think I'm not emotionally there for my children when they need me the most?'

I remember a parent saying,

'As I get the hang of parenting my child, it's as though someone pulls the rug out from under my feet. She moves into a different developmental stage and I start all over again.'

Parenting has enough challenges without us making it more difficult than it needs to be. Focus on how you want to be as a parent, rather than other people's 'shoulds'. This is where the SURE signpost can direct you to notice what does matter and what doesn't. So let's apply SURE to ourselves.

S – Separate out your child's behaviour from your 'Parent' image.

It's so easy when your child acts out to think: 'What will other people say?' / 'My daughter doesn't love me.' / 'I'm not a good enough parent.' If you go down an avenue of negativity, you'll be giving fodder to your reptilian brain, and you'll react rather than respond helpfully. Chasing negative thoughts means you increase your chance of going into a fight or flight reaction, which means you won't connect, and you won't figure out what your child's behaviour is trying to tell you. Choose self-calming strategies and separate out:
'Her behaviour is about her - my response is about me.' [10]

You are choosing to read this book because you know your child's experience matters too. Because you're a regular human being with all the stress being a parent brings, there will be times when you 'flip the lid'. Sometimes you may be so focused on your own agenda, you unthinkingly coerce or manipulate your child. When your child becomes reactive, choose to respond, rather than react. If you react - if you punish, coerce or manipulate - your child will experience 'attack' and will either attack back or go into a defensive shell, which will cut off helpful communication. You won't get the long term result you really want. Rather ask yourself, 'What really matters here?' and you'll discover the helpful way forward. 'HALT be SURE' creates 'win-win' situations, which meet your child's needs as well as your own.

U - Understand your behaviour has a cause and your behaviour has an intention.

It's hard not to berate yourself when you don't parent the way you want to. But most of the times we emotionally hurt our children is when we're in reactive 'crocodile' mode. Understanding your child starts with being understanding towards yourself. Yes, you will lose the cool at times. But the more you become aware, the more you'll notice the signs you're edging towards reaction. When your child behaves in a way that's upsetting, like sticking out her tongue at you, HALT, ask yourself, 'Am I Hungry / Angry/Anxious/ Lonely/ iLL or Tired?' Then you'll be able to pull back from the situation and recognise if there are

10 Tony Humphreys (training course in Univeristy of Cork 2003)

57

other factors at play. You'll be able to calm yourself and give attention to what's needed.

Your behaviour also has an **intention**. In a survive moment it's easy to react. Your reactive intention is probably to 'Restore peace' or 'Teach her to be respectful' - without thinking about the bigger picture. For example, it's easy to tell an older sibling to let the toddler have his toy. But is that helping your child to learn to hold his boundaries? Is it modelling that his needs matter too? Is it teaching him to create a solution where everyone's needs are met, including his own? As parents, we need to hold the bigger, long term picture in mind.

What is your child learning about interactions when you react? When you choose to respond you'll be asking yourself, 'What really matters here?' Then your intention will be to turn this survive moment into a thrive opportunity - to connect with your child because then both you and she will gain the real learning from the incident.

R - Respond from a place of Separateness and Understanding.

When your child acts out, your reactive thoughts can spin out of control. It's easy to make up a story in your head:

'She hates me.' 'She hates her sister.' 'She's a bad child.'

You don't know that these thoughts are true. They are just ideas that run through your head.

Choose to separate from unhelpful thoughts which drive you to react. It's more helpful to ask yourself, 'What might this behaviour be telling me?'

By separating out your child's behaviour is about her and your response is about you, it will be easier to respond from a place of understanding. Think back to Maureen's story about her child sticking out her tongue at her. If Maureen remembers her child's behaviour is about her and her response is about herself, she will keep calm and respond in a way that gives her daughter the opportunity to express her unhappy feelings that lie beneath this behaviour. She will discover what her daughter's experience is; whether she is experiencing Maureen's behaviour as unfair or whether there is some other issue troubling her. When you separate out your unhelpful thoughts from what's needed it will lead you to a place of understanding.

Also separate yourself and your response from what others might think or say.

Imagine, for instance, how much harder it would be for Trish to respond to Alice's upset if her mother-in-law's 'sliding eyebrow' was behind her. You won't be present to yourself or to your child when your attention is focused on what others think. This is your child and your situation. There will always be some people who disapprove of how you handle a situation. It's easy to get hooked into trying to control your child's behaviour because you're worried about other people's opinions. Handling a challenging situation with your child isn't about other people's judgement. This is between you and your child. It's not about what anyone else thinks. Again, ask yourself, 'What really matters here?'

E - Ensure Safety.

Be aware of your own need for emotional safety.

If you react you're likely to end up feeling guilty or upset about your own behaviour.

If you are mindful about how you are, you'll be able to calm your own reactivity and respond helpfully. If you begin to lose your cool, step away from the situation so you can get your 'crocodile' under control. Hurting children (physically or emotionally) is never okay but children are amazingly forgiving. When there's an altercation where you behaved badly, set the example of saying sorry. (Obviously I'm not talking about violence towards your child. Get professional help immediately if you think your child is at risk from anyone, including from yourself).

Apologising when you realise you lost your cool is important not only to restore your relationship but to restore your own inner safety. If you stay upset about the incident you'll increase your stress, which increases the cortisol levels in your body, which trigger your 'crocodile brain', which means you'll lose the cool more easily again! Forgive yourself. Let go of it. Move on. (As toddlers do!) Do what you need to regain your calm. Get back to 'whole-brain mode'. Figure out what you could have done differently so you have greater insight for when a similar incident occurs.

♡

There's one more thing I want to cover in this session,' commented Joy. 'It's my concern our society rewards compliant behaviour. Let me share an incident. I caught a lift with a family with a toddler. This child sat without complaining or calling for any attention for the whole three hour trip, even though he had no books to read or toys to play with, and his mother hardly interacted with him. When we arrived at our destination one of the other passengers complimented the mother on her "well-behaved child." What is your response?' asked Joy.

'My one won't sit still for ten minutes.' said Martin. 'Children have that drive to play. It's so strong they can't ignore it.'

'Sitting still for any length of time isn't natural to a young child,' said Trish.

'So why did he sit still?' queried Maureen. 'Maybe because he's been punished or ignored? He's given up hope that his needs will be met.'

♡

Why 'Always Good' Children Are Cause For Concern

Ironically, society tends to praise the parent whose child is 'good' (in other words, the child who does not interfere with your adult agenda) regardless of the cost for the child. When a child is always compliant with the parent's agenda, when he does not protest at all, be concerned. He may have lost hope he can have his needs met; that he can create the change he needs. When a child's needs are regularly ignored or attacked he may come to believe he is not worth attention and may give up trying. Every child needs to be confident his thoughts, opinions, emotions and experiences matter.

♡

But shouldn't children do what they're told?' asked Martin.

'Yes and no,' responded Joy. 'Let's discuss discipline issues. Tell me what frustrates you about your child.'

They were quick to give examples.

'Not being ready on time.'

'Dawdling.'

'Doesn't tidy her bedroom.'

'Doesn't do his homework.'

'And how do you feel then?' Joy asked.

'Frustrated!' exclaimed the group, with one voice.

'It's easy to react at times, especially if you're under pressure to get to school, to the shop or to your business meeting,' continued Joy. 'You want them to HURRY UP! If you're anything like me, you can be so focused on your need, you forget your child is a person too, and he has his own agenda. You want him to hurry up – he wants play. He is not being naughty – he sees life from a different perspective. He wants to play. He's expressing what's important for him. It's easy to wish for a compliant child, who always does what he is told but a key part of your job as parent is to prepare your child for adult life.

Is compliancy what you want for your child as a mature adult?

Do you want your child to grow up to say yes to whatever is demanded of him? Think about it,' said Joy. 'Imagine your child in adulthood – what if his pals ask him to take drugs, to have sex "because everyone else is doing it", to drive your car without permission. Don't you want your child to know how to say his "no" and mean his "no"? If you want your child to be a competent adult who can respectfully assert what he thinks and believes, and can listen to his own inner voice to make wise choices, then it begins with how he is treated in the home. I believe your role as parent is not to raise a compliant child; but to raise a competent child. One who is able to respond appropriately in different situations; in a way which will not compromise himself or others. He won't always be a model child or always make healthy choices. But every situation is an opportunity to discover what works in life and what doesn't. Every misbehaviour, like your child pulling a face at you, is an invitation to support your child to grow towards competency - to help him to learn to express what he needs and to learn to respond to what others are experiencing. Everyday upsets are your opportunity to support your child to lead the richest, fullest life that is uniquely his.'

Martin looked thoughtful. 'What about our school system? Teachers praise kids' "good behaviour".'

Joy nodded. 'Ironically teachers tend to praise compliant children - the ones who are unquestioningly obedient. Teachers have a challenging task - often too many pupils per class, not enough resources and too much paperwork demanded of them - so they're happy with compliant children. Sadly, many teachers don't have a conscious goal to develop children's social and emotional competency. Think about it - the children who are not easy to parent, the ones who challenge the status quo at home and in the classroom, the ones who don't do as they are told are often the ones who

make the most impact in society as adults.'
Trish laughed. 'Imagine Einstein, Richard Branson or Robin Williams as children! I bet they weren't compliant pupils!'

♡

How to discipline to create meaningful long-term results

You feel frustrated when your child doesn't 'go with the flow' of your agenda. But what if you view your child's protest as an invitation to get to know what matters to him - an opportunity to help him to develop effective negotiation and relationship skills? Notice when your child protests. Look beneath the tantrum, the squabble, or whatever is the behaviour you are focused on. What is he actually asking for? What is the real issue?

When your child plays up, choose to 'listen to the behaviour'. Ask yourself, 'What might my child's behaviour be trying to tell me?'

What is your child's behaviour telling you he needs:

Slowdown time?

More play?

To be treated fairly?

To be listened to?

To be given responsibility?

To be trusted?

It makes sense your child will protest when his agenda doesn't match yours. At times it's possible your children's agenda might be the healthier choice. Your child protests when you squash the fun, when you stop the play, when you insist on seriousness. Maybe more chill out time on your part would not only make home happier, it's possible you would be healthier too. What is the message of your child's protest?

*'Each person is equally a student and a teacher to everyone else. ...
When we accept whomever we're with as our teacher regardless of their behaviour, we see - and act quite differently in – the world.'* [11]

♡

'So do I let my child get away with it?' asked Martin again.

'Give me an example,' replied Joy.

'I tell her to wear this jersey,' said Martin. 'But she replies, "I don't like that jersey."

Or I ask her to sit quietly when we're at the restaurant and she wants to run around and play.'

'So what do you think when that happens?' asked Joy.

'Oh I get frustrated,' said Martin. 'I think she's trying to get at me - to show me I'm not the boss.'

'And when you think those thoughts what happens inside?' asked Joy.

'Ha, my crocodile gets snapping,' laughed Martin. 'Then I can react!'

The group chuckled.

---

11 JAMPOLSKY AND CIRINCIONE, 2008: 120

'So imagine how the situation might be different if you recognise your daughter is not trying to get at you,' said Joy. 'She's not trying to show you who's boss. Rather, she has a different agenda to you. HALT, be SURE. What could that behaviour be telling you?'

Martin reflected, 'Maybe she needs some crayons and paper to keep her busy at the restaurant.'

Joy nodded. 'That doesn't mean you don't set limits. It's bringing us to our third signpost - 'FLAC'. Your child needs you to be in control. To have a home without anyone in control is like a plane flying without a pilot. (And equally awful would be to have a toddler or preschooler as pilot).'

The group smiled.

'I sure need to get a handle on FLAC,' said Martin.

'We'll get there soon enough,' replied Joy, 'but first we need to focus on what we mean by "approach mode" and why it matters.'

♡

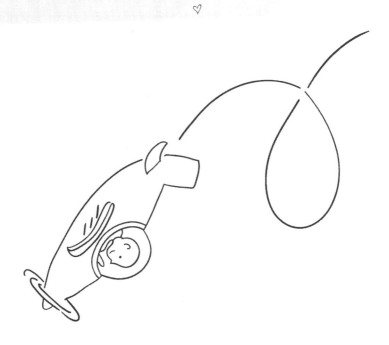

TO SUM UP

Here's an overview of SURE, as it relates to yourself:

S –SEPARATE YOUR CHILD'S BEHAVIOUR FROM YOUR 'PARENT IMAGE'.

Separate out her behaviour is about her and your response is about you.

Separate out your child has his own agenda, which may not run parallel with yours.

Separate out any of your thoughts about the incident, which wind you up and prevent you from connecting with your child's experience. Focus on what matters for your child rather than get caught in what you imagine other people's judgements might be.

Separate your reactive emotions and thoughts from what's needed.

U IS UNDERSTAND.

Understand your behaviour also has a cause and an intention.

Run through HALT in your mind to figure out what might be going on for you.

H - are you hungry? (For food, for adult company, for intellectual stimulation?)

A - Are you angry or anxious?

L - are you lonely or ill?

T - are you tired or do you have a temperature?

The bottom line for a happy family is to understand how to meet every family member's needs, including your own.

R - RESPOND FROM A PLACE OF BEING SEPARATE YET CONNECTED.

Respond from a place of separateness and understanding. Separate out your child's behaviour is about her and your response is about you. When you're aware, you can separate out your reactive emotions and thoughts from what's needed, so you can respond in a way which turns this survive moment into a thrive opportunity.

AND E - ENSURE SAFETY.

Ensure everyone's emotional safety, including your own, because your reactivity will obstruct the long-term result you want. If you lose your cool, apologise for your reactive behaviour so emotional safety is restored.

We're ready to discover the power of our third signpost FLAC, which gives you an effective way to set and hold limits, while building your child's self-esteem. Before we go there, let's look at what might be triggering your child's reactivity. In the next chapter you'll discover how 'Approach Mode' creates the happier outcomes which you and your child would both prefer.

CHAPTER SIX

Choose Approach Mode

Choose Approach Mode

♡

'What you're saying about raising competent children makes sense,' said Maureen. 'But sometimes I ask my child something reasonable and she will not cooperate.'

'Would you be willing to try an experiment?' asked Joy. Trish and the other parents looked at her expectantly. 'I'm going to describe three different scenarios to you. At the end of each I'll ask you to respond with the word: "Ok".

Scenario 1: Imagine your friend has been trying to explain some technical issue and you can't grasp it. At last you understand, and with a happy sigh of relief, you say "OK!"'

Joy waited for them to give their "ok".

'Scenario 2: Your child is nagging and whining at you to do something but you don't want to. You have too much else to be thinking about already. But in the end, out of sheer frustration and for some peace and quiet, you decide it will be easier to go along with his request. You don't want to but you say, "Ok!"'

Joy paused again for the response. This time the "ok" sounded quite different.

'Scenario 3. Your friend asks you if you're free this evening. She has two tickets for your favourite show and she's inviting you out! You're delighted and you say, "OK!"'

Trish laughed as she noticed how their tone of voice, their energy, body language, and facial expression changed in these three different scenarios. They all got it - communicating with your child is more than just the words you use.

♡

Your child is far more tuned in to your body language cues, your tone of voice, the energy with which you say things, than your actual words. She listens to the message beneath your words far more than the words themselves. The cortex, the reasoning part of the brain, is still under construction, so your young child relies far more on visual and 'body-felt' cues in interactions than you do as an adult. Even as adults we are highly sensitive to tone of voice, eye contact, energy levels and body language. So focusing only on the words you use is not going to give you the results you want.

♡

Maureen's brow crinkled slightly. 'So when my child is resistant, even if I think I'm being reasonable, maybe she's getting some other message from me?'
'It's possible,' said Joy. 'Imagine seeing the situation through her eyes. How would she experience your body language and facial expression; your tone of voice?'
'So my nonverbal communication contributed to what unfolded!'
Joy smiled.

♡

As a busy parent, often juggling different needs and priorities, it makes sense you can easily focus on your own agenda. You won't manage to be mindful all the time, but you can become more aware of how your child experiences you. Love and Stosny state all behaviours have one of three motivations. You either avoid, attack or approach[12]. Whenever your child registers you are in avoid or attack mode it triggers the reptilian part of his brain and he will react to you. When he senses you are in approach mode he will respond in a 'whole-brain engaged' cooperative way. When you are in approach mode your child cooperates because he does not sense his needs or way of seeing things is under threat. When you are in approach mode your child gets the message, 'You matter.' Then he can respond and cooperate with you. Let's take a look at these three different modes.

---

12 LOVE AND STOSNY, 2007:168

Recognise Your Mode of Behaviour

Avoid

You probably recognise your own variation of avoid. Different parents avoid in different ways -

physically leaving the space,
disappearing behind the newspaper, book or laptop.
You possibly also avoid by changing the subject or by attending to some task or somebody else's need.
You avoid when you ignore your child's behaviour, his opinion, experience or feelings.

Trish was surprised when Jim, the quiet one in the group, suddenly spoke.
'I get what you're saying about avoid behaviour,' he said.
'The other evening our John, who's six now, appeared at the door. He was speaking in an irritating, whiny voice and he looked as though he was about to start crying.
'The stupid computer game won't work!" he blurted.
My wife was busy making the meal so she said,

"Well, you've been on the computer long enough. It's supper now."
That was all she said - but he went into total meltdown. I was annoyed with him because I thought he was acting like a baby. I'm thinking about it now and I can see we were avoiding his experience. No wonder he reacted.'

'Okay,' Joy responded. 'Would you be willing to role play being your son and I'll be you? Let's take a rerun, choosing approach mode instead.'

Jim nodded. He went and stood at the door, looking towards Joy. In a plaintive, six year old voice he whined, 'The computer game won't work!'

Joy (role-playing the parent) stopped the 'cooking' and moved towards him, giving him her full attention: 'You're upset it won't work. Do you want help?'

Jim broke out of the role-play.

'Wow.' He said. 'I felt felt [13]. Like you cared. No wonder John reacted!'

Joy asked what they noticed in the role play.

'When John experienced his parent reflecting his words and empathising with him, he felt heard,' said Trish.

Joy nodded. 'John's stressed tone of voice and the brimming eyes, which Jim noticed, indicate he was close to emotional flooding, but when the child feels felt (when somebody responds sympathetically to his emotions), he'll calm down. The emotional flooding subsides and the thinking part of his brain can re-engage. Only when the reasoning part of his brain reconnects will he be able to think reflectively and be able to cooperate with his parent's agenda. He's not being unreasonable on purpose - rather he's unreason-able - unable to reason - when he's distressed, until he gets the emotional support he needs to calm down.'

Sometimes when you empathise with your child, the tears will suddenly start to flow. The tears we cry when we peel an onion are chemically different to the tears we cry when we're emotionally upset[14] (because these tears contain stress hormones). The tears are a release, which help your child regain his equilibrium.

---

13 THE EXPRESSION 'FEEL FELT' IS A TERM USED IN RELATIONSHIP THEORY. IT INDICATES THE EXPERIENCE OF ONE'S EMOTIONS BEING ACKNOWLEDGED.

14 WWW.DRJUDITHORLOFF.COM/FREE-ARTICLES/THE-HEALTH-BENEFITS-OF-TEARS_COPY.HTM 12 OCTOBER 2014

♡

'But doesn't a boy need to toughen up?' asked Martin.

Trish sighed. It could have been her husband talking.

'The interesting thing is,' replied Joy, 'the reverse is true. As your child gets older, if he's experienced empathetic parenting he'll learn to express his emotions appropriately. On the other hand, if his inner experience is repeatedly ignored, he'll be likely to operate in survive mode and he'll be reactive. A person who has not experienced emotional connection in the developing years will either find it hard to express emotion or else will be over-reactive. The good news is that Emotional Intelligence is not permanently fixed by our earlier experiences. We can develop it at any age. We can learn how to contain our emotions appropriately and have free flowing relationships, even if we didn't have the emotional connection we needed as children. Emotionally connected people contain themselves appropriately. They are more resilient and have a network of support. So emotionally connected children are strong on the inside, rather than having a tough shell that often is hiding an inner vulnerabilty, like a tortoise. When children consistently experience emotional connection they develop the ability to make a connected whole-brain-engaged response in stressful situations.'

Jim looked thoughtful. 'Ok. Fast forward fifteen years. If we've given John the emotional support you're describing, what might his response be?'

'Anybody want to try?' asked Joy.

Trish felt excited. She got it. When things go wrong, no need to start shouting. No need to blame or shame anyone else. This was making sense to her.

'I'll try,' she said.

'Ok - now you're John, aged twenty-one and the computer programme won't load.' prompted Joy.

Trish cleared her throat, and spoke in a clear, firm voice: 'I'm feeling frustrated with this computer game.'

The group laughed and cheered.

♡

72

When tempers are frayed or when you're over-tired, you might sometimes choose avoid mode rather than enter into a difficult debate. And sometimes that can be the more helpful short-term approach, until you have had a chance to regain your inner balance. But when you resort to 'avoid' behaviours your child is likely to protest, often by acting out. Perhaps your child will subconsciously prefer your scolding, (at least you're connecting with him), than your withdrawal. Any attention can feel better than no attention.

If you regularly choose avoid mode there will be a price to pay - it's going to affect family relationships. If you repeatedly avoid, your child might act out more to get you to reengage, or over time she might lose hope her needs will be met, and cope with her loss of your connectedness in some other way. She might become over-absorbed in her schoolwork or a hobby, or put all her energy and attention into a friendship, at the expense of your relationship.

What about time-out strategies, such as a naughty chair or sending

him to his room? Your child will experience your behaviour as avoid. It might appear to work because, as parent, you achieve what you want - but ask yourself, 'At what cost?' If your child on a regular basis experiences you as avoiding her, how does this impact her self worth? What does this do to her sense of personal agency (her sense of being able to create healthy change in what's happening in her life)? This can cause her to believe she is powerless to bring change in relationship. Think how important it is to know, 'I can express what I need and be heard' in all your relationships - at home and at work. Being heard and feeling felt affects our sense of well-being.

When a child is punished by being isolated until she 'says sorry' (whether the bold step, the naughty corner or sent to her room) the message she's probably getting is,

'Unless you do what I want you to do, and think the way I think you should think, I will withhold my love from you.'

There will be a cost when a child repeatedly feels powerless to reconnect with you - when she feels she has to let go of her needs and her experience, to reconnect with you. She might stop believing in herself as being a person who matters, and go with whatever others expect of her, no matter whether it feels good or bad to her. Or she might become willful and obstinate; ignoring anything other than what she wants, as a way of holding on to her sense of self.

Imagine this in her adult life with an intimate other. She might be so afraid of being disconnected from that person she will deny her own needs, and be open to being abused. She may react on the other extreme, by 'freezing out' the other person whenever there's a disagreement, (in other words using an adult version of 'sending you to the naughty corner' against people who don't go with her agenda). Either way, regular use of avoid behaviours with your child is likely to cause future pain in how your child learns to deal with challenging interpersonal situations. You lose the opening to turn your child's survive moments into thrive opportunities, where your child can learn from the experience.

Attack

When you are calm and collected, you probably rationally agree you are not likely to get the results you want, when you attack your children. Attack behaviours, like shouting, smacking or nagging, will trigger your child's reptilian brain, causing a fear reaction. Attack behaviours will be punishing, rather than helpful discipline. Smacking, shouting and other forms of punishment trigger a sense of fear or anxiety in your child, which will cause him to react to keep himself safe. The crocodile brain triggers a fight, flight, freeze, or appease reaction.

When your child experiences you in attack mode he might:

FIGHT - attack back, either verbally or physically.
(e.g. tell you 'You're stupid,' or 'I hate you.')

FLIGHT - perhaps run out the room or to another adult, or totally absorb in some activity, e.g. stare at the television.

FREEZE - stop doing everything, then maybe your attention will turn elsewhere.

APPEASE - your child complies; he does whatever you want but shuts off his own thoughts or feelings or experiences.

Your attack mode might get the immediate behaviour you want - but it will be from your child's reaction to keep himself out of danger. This means, because he is purely reacting from his 'crocodile brain', there will be no worthwhile 'whole brain engaged' learning which your child will take to use in other similar situations.

If your child is reactive, even though you didn't think you were in attack mode, pause to imagine how your interaction could be seen from your child's point of view. You probably don't intend to attack or avoid your child but how your child experiences you is going to cause a reaction or a response. Sometimes, your child will react if he experiences your timing is off. You walk in the door with a pleasant tone of voice and a smile, but the first thing you say is, 'Have you done your homework?' Then you think your child is 'in a bad mood' / 'acting like a brat' when he back-chats you, or reacts in some other way. But every one of us needs to be seen and valued for who we are. Imagine if your significant other hasn't seen you for several hours and the first words of greeting you receive are:
'Did you pay the bills?' or 'Did you get the car fixed?'
Wouldn't you react angrily? You might think,
'Don't I matter?'
Your child will react to how she experiences you. If you don't see her, if you dominate or threaten, she will register your mode as attack. She will also experience your manipulation or coercion as attack. Imagine these comments from your child's perspective:
'Don't you think it's time to do your homework now?'
'Won't you be a good girl and share with your sister?'
When you think your child is behaving unreasonably, or being uncooperative, ask yourself if she's experiencing your behaviour as attack. The more you insist the more she will resist.

When your child experiences your attack or avoid, she might answer you back, argue, sulk, refuse to cooperate, or get into a fight with you or with a sibling. All these behaviours make sense when you recognise your behaviour has been experienced as attack or avoid. This has triggered a reaction in your child.

Imagine hearing 'Haven't you done your homework?' through her ears instead of yours. How would you experience that if you were your child? Your child will react if she experiences you as coercive. She is far more likely to respond once you have already connected and when you give clear, direct communication, which doesn't disempower:
'Remember we agreed homework time is from five to six o'clock.'
Likewise, demands for your child to share her toy are likely to be stonewalled. Rather use a comment which encourages creative cooperation:
'I see you want to play with your toy. What can we do to keep your little sister happy?'

The alternative to avoid or attack is approach. When you consistently respond from an inner place of love and connection, your body will naturally transmit an approach mode; you'll create connection and meaningful communication, which will naturally lead to cooperation.

Approach
Your child will experience approach when you desire to:
- Connect with her,
- Discover more and learn more about her and her perspective
- Appreciate her just for who she is. [15]

When your child feels approached she will sense you are genuinely interested in her and how she is experiencing the situation. If you have

15 LOVE AND STOSNY 2007: 169

a young child, even though she won't be able to put the experience into words she will be sensitive to your avoid, attack or approach mode. You will recognise this by the response or reaction you receive from her.

Trish rubbed her eyes. It had been a long day. The baby had woken before five and so Alice had decided it was time to get up too. When Trish insisted she go back to bed Alice had burst into tears. That was the end of sleep for any of them. Trish was glad this evening's Parenting session was nearly finished so she could soon get some sleep.

Joy's words jolted her back in the group.

'Take time to notice when you are calm, collected and centred on creating more enjoyable and fulfilling family life, where everyone's needs (including yours) are taken into account. Notice what happens to family dynamics when you approach. Choose words to describe your emotional experience at this time and notice how your body feels. Notice the quality of the space between you.'

'Approach mode' thought Trish. 'I'm normally so busy barking the orders, I don't even think about how I come across to the kids or to Derek. Alice is giving me such a hard time because she wants me to connect with her!'

Trish could hardly wait to see what happened when she focused on approach.

♡

In approach mode you are in an open, accepting, present heartspace and headspace. You listen to your child's experience or opinion. You feel compassionate towards her, even if you have a different opinion or don't understand her perspective. Being in approach mode with your child is about trust, and the result is togetherness, connection, communication and love.

When you are in approach mode, the reptilian part of your child's brain is not triggered, (and neither is yours). If your child is already upset, and you are in a calm approach space your child is far more likely to become calm again, because emotions are contagious. Even if your child is distressed, your approach presence reduces feelings of fear or shame, so a sense of well-being is quickly restored.

When you create emotional safety for your child - when he feels felt, his

reactivity will subside and then he will be able to make a whole-brain response. He'll be able to connect to his emotions and to the logic part of the brain. Your empathy and validation of his experience helps him to process difficult or painful situations. In other words, even in minor situations, like John's frustration with the computer, if he consistently experiences a safe space to work through strong emotions, other similar situations won't trigger a reptilian brain reaction. Rather, he'll be able to make a reasoned response. Imagine the difference in his adult life as a partner, as a parent, as a work colleague or a boss. Being in approach mode with your child, as far as you possibly can, might be one of the greatest gifts you ever give him.

To sum up

Whenever you attempt to control your child you are likely to trigger a reptilian brain reaction, which means you are not going to achieve the long-term results you desire. If you are both reactive, things easily spin out of control into power struggles and conflict. Rather than reacting in ways which your child may experience as avoid or attack, respond in a way which your child will experience as approach, which will, over time, create cooperation.

Even when you have developed the skill of approach, there will still be times when your child tests the limits. In the next chapter you'll discover FLAC. This amazingly simple signpost will preserve your sanity when your child is wrecking your home or wrecking your head, because you will be able to set limits without shouting, threatening or nagging.

CHAPTER SEVEN

Use 'FLAC' to Set Limits

Use 'FLAC' to Set Limits

♡

Trish hummed to herself as she packed the supper dishes into the dishwasher. She glanced at her watch. Enough time to pop on her pretty new blouse before Pam came to collect her.

'Oh Derek, please don't forget to check Jamie's spellings. She's got a test tomorrow.'

'Fine.' snarled Derek. His 'fine' sounded anything but fine. Trish stopped in her tracks.

'What's up with him?' She's been so wrapped up thinking about the evening ahead, she hadn't noticed he was out of sorts.

He hadn't talked while they were clearing the dishes away but she thought he was just tired from work. Things were challenging since the economic downturn.

'I don't know why you're wasting your time doing this parenting course,' he blurted. 'What's wrong with the way our parents raised us!'

Before Trish could answer he stormed out the room.

Time was running out. If she didn't get ready now she'd miss her lift.

She battled to stop the tears as she touched up her mascara.

What exactly was eating him? But she didn't have time now.

The doorbell rang and she went downstairs to answer it.

She kissed the kids and shouted 'bye' to Derek, but only a frosty silence answered. She forced a smile as she greeted Pam, not wanting her to see she was upset.

'He might not see the value of it,' she thought, as they drove towards the centre, 'but I'm already seeing how this course is shifting my thinking in a more helpful direction.'

She felt despondent as she walked into the meeting that evening but soon she was focused on the story she was hearing.

'We were coming out of the supermarket. The trolley's laden with a full week's groceries and our three year old starts performing:

"I want my new toy."

I say to him. "No – not now Johnny. Wait till we get home."

'I want my toy." Johnny starts winding up the volume and pitch.
"I want my toy."
 Everyone in the carpark is staring at us and Johnny gets louder and louder - wailing and carrying on until he's in a full blown tantrum.
I couldn't stand it. I stopped right there and delved through the mounds of shopping until I found the toy. He wouldn't stop crying till I let him have it.
What could I have done differently?'
'Guess what's going to happen next time you go shopping!' laughed Martin. 'He knows it worked this time so he's bound to repeat the performance next time!'
'I heard you say you told him to wait until you're home.' Joy paused and then she shared a joke:
'The duck waddles into the hardware store and asks the shopkeeper.
"Ya got any gwapes?"
"Nope." replies the shopkeeper - and out waddles the duck!
A few minutes later the duck returns.
"Ya got any gwapes?"
"Nope." replies the shopkeeper - and out waddles the duck. Again the duck comes in:
"Ya got any gwapes?"
"Nope." replies the shopkeeper - and out waddles the duck! Eventually when the duck asks
"Ya got any gwapes?" The shopkeeper fumes,
"Now listen here, duck, you come in here asking for grapes one more time, and I'm gonna nail your flat feet to the floor."
Out waddles the duck. A few minutes later he's back again:
"Ya got any nails?"
"Nope." replies the shopkeeper.
"Ya got any gwapes?"'

Like the duck, your child will test you to see if you mean what you say. When you cave in even once, or state consequences your child knows you won't follow through, you set yourself up for more of the same nagging, whining or other annoying behaviour.

In this chapter you'll discover how to use FLAC to set limits; a useful signpost when your child tries to insist on you meeting his wants.

With FLAC you can create more peace in the home, and support your child's sense of himself and his ability to make choices. It's a helpful tool to use with children old enough to articulate their choices, usually about their third year. FLAC is not suitable for toddlers because the brain is still 'under construction'[16] and they are not able to deal adequately with choices yet, especially at times when they may be upset or stressed. FLAC is only suitable to use with children who have well-developed language skills to make reasoned choices.

Before we go any further, a reminder: HALT be SURE before you use FLAC.

HALT be SURE - respond to what's going on for your child, which will often dissolve the behaviour issue you are dealing with. When you can recognise and respond to what your child needs (rather than reacting to what he wants) it often deactivates the stressful situation. Use HALT to make a quick assessment, 'Is he hungry, angry, anxious, lonely, ill or tired?' and respond to any need. 'H' is also a reminder for 'Thirsty?' as well as 'Hungry?' So perhaps he needs a drink of water or something to eat to help him regain calm. This makes sense because if your child's blood sugar levels are low he's more likely to be cranky and fractious.[17] Having something to eat can avoid a meltdown. With HALT you can figure out what is needed.

At other times, as with the child coming out from the supermarket, you may know he's tired but you still want to hold the limit you set. In an ideal world we would communicate adequately to dissolve any challenge in the relationship. But as parents we don't always have the inner resources or the time to navigate the twists and turns of an upset at that particular moment. You might be tired too and there's

16 See Sunderland 2006:20-25 for greater detail about this.
17 Sunderland 2006: 113

a trolley-load of groceries to be taken home and unpacked. Check in with HALT for yourself - are you hungry, anxious or angry or tired? If so, then you can easily react, which won't be helpful. If you've dealt with the practical HALT issues but know you aren't in a good place to listen well, it's probably more helpful to use FLAC to keep a limit rather than risk you also becoming reactive. When you both become reactive your 'crocodiles get to tango' and things will go from bad to worse!

So here's what to do when your child is insisting on what he wants and you are striving to hold a limit. Use FLAC to maintain the boundary.

You know the expression 'Don't give me flac.'

We tend to use it when we mean,

'Don't give me a hard time.'

I was told by an old soldier it was an expression used in the last World War.

It was used to describe 'friendly fire' - when troops accidentally fired at their own aircraft. FLAC is a reminder you are on the same side as your child. You are not enemies. This does not have to be a power struggle. So let's take a look at this signpost.

F - state **Feelings**
L - set **Limit**
A - give **Alternatives**
C - state **Consequence** of the child's choice

♡

Joy asked the group for a practical example of a time where the child was pushing the limits, where FLAC could be helpful.

Tom spoke 'This week our four year old has taken to writing on the walls.'

They quickly ran through 'HALT' - Hungry? Angry? Anxious? Lonely or ILL? Tired or Temperature? Tom couldn't identify any pressing concerns and he sensed this behaviour was purely a curiosity about writing on a different surface.

Maureen suggested taping a large sheet of paper on the wall for art work, but Tom would still need to set the limit.

So Joy led them through using FLAC.

Start with the 'F' for Feelings. State what you know she'd like to do.

(Use her name to get her attention).

"Jenny, I know you'd like to write on the walls."

'L' - State the Limit.

"But walls are not for writing on."

'A' - Give her the Alternatives.

"You can choose to write on the paper or you can choose for the crayons to be put away."

Finally 'C' - state the Consequence which she has chosen.

"So I see you chose to write on the paper,"

or

"So I see you chose for the crayons to be put away."

Joy emphasised the wording of the consequence:

'Please note you do not say,

"So I'm putting the crayons away."

*Rather word it, "So **you** chose the crayons are put away."*

The sense of power remains with her. It was HER choice.'

By calmly stating the choice your child has made, you are helping her to realise she can make choices and she will have to take the consequences of her choice. An important life lesson every child needs to absorb.

Here's how to use FLAC:

F - Acknowledge What Your Child is Feeling.

Acknowledge his experience in that moment. This gives your child the message you understand and it acknowledges his viewpoint.

e.g. 'I know you would like to ...'

L - Clearly State the Limit.

State the behaviour that you expected. Don't use any extra words. This is the same objective limit which applies to everyone all the time (like the speed limit on the road).

For example, 'We walk inside the shop.'

'People are not for hurting.' (or expressed positively, 'Gentle hands.')

A - Give the Alternatives.

This is the hardest part. It takes practise to think of alternatives which are an obvious and fair consequence to the situation. An alternative must always give a choice. To say, 'You can do it or not' is not a choice. Also, make sure you give alternatives you are prepared to carry through and which 'make sense' to the child in that context. One mother in a parenting course said she would say,

'So you can choose to get dressed or you can choose to go to school in your pyjamas.'

I would not use that choice because I would never be able to follow through and let my child go to school in pyjamas. You know yourself. Don't give an alternative unless you are prepared to follow through. Imagine how this would (or wouldn't) make sense to your child. Giving a choice of the crayons being put away, when writing on the walls is the issue, makes sense to the child. Sometimes I've heard parents say something like,

'So you can choose to eat your food or you can choose for your doll to be taken away.'

But what is the connection between the doll and the food? Taking a beloved toy away might make an easy choice for you but ask yourself,

'Does this choice make sense or seem fair in this situation to my child?'

Imagine how you would feel if things you loved were removed from you if you didn't comply! That's coercing - using your power over the child in a way which creates fear or anxiety - not a form of discipline where there are natural, acceptable consequences.

C - State the Consequence Your Child Chooses.

When you state the consequence the child has chosen, it is essential you follow through because if you don't you will revert to the old power struggle. Your child will push to see if your limits are firm.

FLAC creates a calmer, happier home - provided you always follow through.

Your child must know when you give a choice - that's it. You will not back down or alter the rules.

If your child refuses to make a choice then you say,

'If you don't make a choice then you choose for me to make the choice for you.'

♡

Joy shared an example.

'Jane and her friend begin to chat when Jane's children start a game of chase around the kitchen table. Jane doesn't want an upset with her friend present – so, in an effort to calm the children, she says to the children, "Ok now."

When the children carry on, Jane tries to ignore it. The children tear around the table, laughing and shouting to each other. Jane and her friend can't enjoy a relaxed chat together. Eventually Jane's patience runs out.

"Out, out!" she roars - chasing the children out of the house.

Result – the children are unhappy. Jane is disappointed and so is her friend.'

'Now,' said Joy, 'Let's re-run the scenario, using FLAC.

The children begin to run around the table. Jane senses herself feeling frustrated. She stops the children.

She talks calmly (she can keep her calm because she's setting limits early – rather than wait until she's steaming!)

She states the Feeling.

"I know you'd like to run around the table."

Then she sets the Limit.

"But the kitchen is for walking only."

Then she gives the Alternative,

"So you can choose to sit and play quietly or you can choose to go and run outside."

Finally she states the Consequence:

"So you have chosen to go run outside," (calmly opening the door!)

Or, if they settle, "So you have chosen to play quietly in the kitchen."

(With her tone of voice and eyes affirming their co-operative behaviour.)

Result: Jane has a peaceful cup of tea with her friend and nobody is upset or feels disrespected.'

'Yes,' thought Trish. 'I know there are times when Alice pushes me to set a limit. Just wait, little lady, your mummy's going to handle this differently from now on.'

♡

FLAC works when you apply it consistently. But always 'HALT be SURE' before you use FLAC. If your child has an unmet need, like hunger for play, and you try to use FLAC to uphold boundaries in a way that doesn't give him a choice where he can release the energy of his need to play, you are likely to face strong resistance. Think of Joy's example with the children running around the kitchen table. Their play drive was high, she gave them a choice where they could run outside to release that energy. If the challenge is about energetic behaviour, make sure you are asking yourself 'Is he Hungry for play?' When your child is acting out, scan your mind over the day to assess if there has been adequate opportunity for play. Give a way for your child to release play energy, even if it's through a FLAC choice.

What amazes me is how children learn to use FLAC. Often I have parents telling me how they hear their older children giving choices to their younger siblings. How empowering for them - they learn to set non-violent, respectful boundaries for themselves instead of fighting.

Finally in this chapter, let's take a look at a few practical pointers about using FLAC to move discipline in a helpful direction.

FLAC: Practical Pointers

Obviously there are times as a parent when something is a non-negotiable. If it is a potential emergency you need to take immediate action. If your child is about to put his finger in the electricity socket, you act immediately.

You don't say,

'I know you'd like to put your finger in the socket ...!'

This is not a time for FLAC. Take immediate action if this is a safety issue.

If your child is unwell, overtired or overstressed, you need to gently and firmly take control of the situation for everyone's welfare.

Perhaps you are late home and it is cold and wet and you want to get your child quickly inside, even though he wants to walk.

"I know you'd like to walk up the stairs but it's late and I choose to carry you.'

In these circumstances there is no debate. You choose and follow through the course of action. You can say something like,

'So do you want to carry Teddy or leave Teddy in the car?'

This often diffuses the potential power struggle because when you give your child even a small choice you give him some measure of control in the situation.

And remember 'HALT be SURE before you use FLAC.'
HALT - stop before engaging. Ask yourself,
'Is my child
Hungry
Angry /Anxious
Lonely /iLL
or **Tired?** (Or am I?)
When you deal with these questions first, often the issue will dissolve.

Then be SURE. Separate out his behaviour from his person (and from your own reactiveness). Seek to first Understand the behaviour and Respond to what is needed. Before you use FLAC, ask yourself if the limit is reasonable from your child's perspective. If you have been window shopping for the last three hours with your toddler strapped in the pushchair, it makes sense he's cranky. He is hungry for some activity. Try to see the situation through your child's eyes. Rather than trying to impose a limit, respond to his legitimate need.

Ensure both physical and emotional safety for all.

♡

It was a week since Joy introduced FLAC. They were nearing the end of the programme. Tomorrow evening would be the last session.

But Trish had been amused and a little amazed by what had happened yesterday.

She's been in the study and Derek was in the garden with the children. She couldn't hear every word, but she knew by the raised voices that a squabble was about to erupt.

Then she heard Derek's voice calmly say,

'So, Jamie, you can choose to play with the Lego in the house or you can choose for the Lego to be put away.'

Trish couldn't believe it. Derek refused to talk with her about the Parenting programme but now she heard him use FLAC to set a limit with Jamie.

They hadn't discussed it but he must have seen it working when she used it with the kids. Perhaps they'd end up on the same parenting page after all!

♡

TO SUM UP

In this chapter we've looked at FLAC to create effective discipline. Use FLAC to create consistent boundaries by giving your child appropriate choices which ensure everyone's well-being. With FLAC your child learns there are natural consequences to every choice.

FLAC ensures everyone's rights and needs are respected, creating happier more peaceful homes. FLAC helps to build your child's self esteem as he has a sense of agency in the outcome. He's not a helpless victim who has no choice in what happens. This increases his competence and his confidence.

And you are giving your child one of the most important life tools he will ever need, because effective discipline guides your child towards self-discipline. When you model FLAC your child is also absorbing a tool he can use in other life situations to hold his own boundaries in a respectful way. Your child is learning a way to firmly stand for what he needs without letting himself be steamrollered into going with someone else's undesirable agenda and without resorting to aggressive behaviour or meltdown. FLAC will help your child to develop his competence, to grow to be the awesome, joyful adult he is capable of being.

When you have a handle on FLAC, you'll soon be able to use these three signposts to create a more helpful direction in your parenting: HALT be SURE before you use FLAC.

In this chapter we've looked at how to discipline. In the next chapter we'll chat about practical issues - how to respond when your child won't eat or sleep, and the reason FLAC works. We'll also look at the big question of why punishment is not okay and what makes discipline so different.

Here's an overview of the FLAC signpost:

F - ACKNOWLEDGE YOUR CHILD'S FEELING /EXPERIENCE.
L - STATE THE LIMIT.
A - GIVE THE ALTERNATIVES.
C - STATE THE CONSEQUENCE / THE CHOICE YOUR CHILD MAKES.

CHAPTER EIGHT

FLAC - from your perspective

FLAC - from your perspective

Pam started the conversation.

'Sometimes I feel guilty I'm not doing the loving thing when I stick to my limits. I mean, surely if I love my child, I'll give her what she wants.'

*Joy responded, 'It's helpful to separate out your child's wants from needs. Like the story we shared last week, the child may want the toy - and there might be good reason why you want him to wait. But **needs** and **wants** are not the same. He **wants** the toy. He **needs** to still experience connection and support from you, even when you set the limit.'*

Trish and several others nodded.

'If you lived in a perfect world, you would have such great communication with your child you would ideally solve all the challenges without ever needing to use discipline tactics. Perhaps that day will come in future generations, but in our present situation, there will be times when you need to use discipline to set and hold a clear boundary.'

♡

In this chapter we'll chat about the value of FLAC. We'll also reflect on the difference between punishment and discipline and why this matters. FLAC gives your child the opportunity to make choices and to experience the natural consequences of her own actions. When your child is given fair choices, she won't feel like a victim. She will develop a solid sense of her self-esteem when her experience of life is affirmed. (You do this through the 'F' of FLAC - 'I know you'd like to ....' In other words her emotions and thoughts are also acknowledged). FLAC creates effective discipline that respects both your child's needs and yours.

As your child notices you parenting differently he might test you. It's as though he is thinking,

'Is Mum/Dad for real? Let's see!'

If you don't have a clear direction of how to set the limit, you'll try to be 'nice' until you are tested beyond the point where you can keep your cool. Your stress level builds and builds, your crocodile brain is triggered, then - Ka-POW. You turn into the raging monster. Your child will think the 'nice' Mum or Dad was a farce -and it will be hard to regain the ground you have worked so hard to gain.

Welcome to the real world of imperfect and often challenging parenting where children do test the boundaries.

'A child will kick until he feels the walls.' Haim Ginott

FLAC gives you a practical discipline strategy to keep the children (and yourself) safe when they test the limit. And they will test the limit - because children do.

Scott Peck's definition of love can help us to see the importance of limit-setting more clearly:

*'Love is extending yourself
to cause the other person's growth.'* [18]

When you give in to the tantrum and let your child have what he demands you are not extending yourself to cause his growth. He needs to learn other people's needs and agenda are important too. When he learns to wait for what he wants in life, he learns 'delayed gratification' - an important part of maturity.[19] Helping your child to cooperate with

18 ADAPTED - SCOTT PECK HTTP://WWW.GOODREADS.COM/WORK/QUOTES/2747475-THE-ROAD-LESS-TRAVELED-A-NEW-PSYCHOLOGY-OF-LOVE-TRADITIONAL-VALUES-A 1/11/2014
19 ADAPTED - SCOTT PECK HTTP://WWW.GOODREADS.COM/WORK/QUOTES/2747475-THE-ROAD-LESS-TRAVELED-A-NEW-PSYCHOLOGY-OF-LOVE-TRADITIONAL-VALUES-A 1/11/2014

other people's needs and to delay gratification is extending yourself to cause his growth to being a caring and self-disciplined person. So discipline is part of loving your child. How is this extending yourself? Because sometimes it's tough to face your child's anger at you when you are not letting him have his wants. As a loving parent, you extend yourself (even risking being the 'bad guy' in your child's eyes for a while) to develop your child's maturity.

The challenge is to set the limit, in the heat of the moment, in a way that treats your child, and yourself, with respect. This is why a having a reliable tool you can depend on is essential.

To use FLAC effectively, you need practise.

The hardest part of FLAC is giving choices which your child will see as fair consequences, so think about creating a buddy system, whether it's a good friend or your spouse. Your buddy is someone you can chat with about using FLAC appropriately. Your buddy needs to also be fully aware of 'HALT be SURE' because using FLAC will not work unless you have first responded to your child's needs. Your buddy can support you in thinking about appropriate and fair choices, even if it's only after an event, so that you will be better prepared for future situations when your child tests the limits. A buddy isn't necessarily in the home with you. You might connect by phone or internet but it's someone who can support you and remind you to follow the steps of FLAC.

And place the FLAC signpost somewhere at home as a visual reminder.

♡

'It's not that easy,' exclaimed Maureen. 'I want to be understanding and sympathetic to my child. But there's times when she wants things HER way. I try to HALT and be SURE - to take her experience into account too. The thing is, I have an agenda too - I have to drop the kids to school, to get to work, to figure out what we're having for supper. There are times when I can't do things the way my child wants me to. Besides, even if I did have a husband or someone else to help me, I want her to re-alise the world doesn't revolve around her; other people have needs too.' Several people nodded.

'Actually,' said Joy, 'that's exactly why you do need FLAC. It's going to be harder at first but in the long run, your child will know you say what

you mean and mean what you say.'
Martin came in on the conversation,
'I've got a handle on this but what if ...
he won't eat?
he won't go to sleep?

What if your child refuses to eat? When you're feeling stressed, when you're worried about your child eating enough, you probably sometimes forget you cannot control any human being - not even your own child. Even young children want to make their own choices; it's part of our human nature. You cannot make your child eat. Your child has his own inbuilt digestive clock and he will eat when he is hungry. Fussing over your child's eating can cause stress in your relationship. Rather, use 'HALT be SURE' to figure out what might be going on for your child. Maybe he's hungry for your attention. Give your attention in other more helpful ways, perhaps a longer, cuddlier chat at bedtimes, rather than make a fuss about eating. Even a small thing, like making loving eye contact more frequently, can make a surprisingly big difference to your child's demand for attention. Then relax about the food issue. You can't force your child to eat but you can provide healthy food choices and expect your child to sit at the table while the family eats. Providing you've taken time to HALT and be SURE everything is okay, and he isn't being allowed to eat whatever else or whenever else he wants to, it's likely he will soon join in at mealtimes.

Likewise, you cannot make your child sleep. Check HALT to figure out if there's anything of concern. The 'A - is he Anxious?' is often triggered at bedtime, especially if he hasn't had enough connect time with you. Things look different in the dark; car lights and shadows can become scary monsters. School or separation issues can loom threateningly. Only when you have taken time to 'HALT be SURE' can you expect him to be quiet and settled.

What about the times your child seems to push the limits for the sake of pushing the limits? What do you do? First, your child needs limits. A world without any boundaries is a scary place for a child to be. A home without limits is like a house without walls - nothing in place to keep your child safe when he needs it most. Setting fair, consistent limits is part of loving your child. That doesn't mean your child will like you setting limits, but when you have made regular deposits of unconditional love, trust, caring and respect, the times when you use FLAC to set firm, fair boundaries will not bankrupt your relationship.

Why Does FLAC Work?

FLAC works because you give your child a choice. This relieves her feelings of frustration, which is often because she feels powerless. I think many fairy tales have giants in them because children often feel as though we adults are giants - choosing to do whatever we will and leaving them feeling unsafe, helpless and frustrated.

♡ FLAC gives a choice - when your child has a choice she is no longer powerless, so her anger often dissipates.
♡ FLAC sets clear limits, so everyone knows where they stand.
♡ FLAC means you can choose to deal with the situation before people become out-of-control angry and unreason-able (unable to reason).

Feelings of anger start with mild irritation, or frustration. Gradually you become cross, and if the source of irritation is not dealt with, your feelings spiral downwards into rage. Now your crocodile brain is in control. You can't make the helpful choices you would like.
Think of the expressions we use to describe extreme anger:
'in a blind fury,'
'all steamed up',
' raging mad.'
You can't see clearly when you're mad. You can't think straight when you are furious. Small incidents spiral out of control and become major

upsets. So what helps you to handle your anger differently? Become aware of the first sensations of frustration in your body. Perhaps your jaw tightens, or your body temperature increases. Perhaps you notice your voice getting louder or higher. Now is the time to take action, before you lose your cool and the crocodile brain takes charge. Whilst you can still think clearly and reason-ably, pay attention to your body's early-warning anger signals. Rather than letting your anger build to the point where you react, choose to respond. Listen to what both your anger and your child's anger might be trying to tell you.

Ask yourself:

'What change is needed here?'

HALT be SURE to figure out what response is needed. If you need to set the limit, use FLAC before angry feelings escalate. This matters because if feelings of anger or fear are raging, you are more likely to punish than to discipline, which won't build connection and cooperation. Ask yourself, 'What is the end result I really want?'

♡

The group were talking about how to discipline children. Trish was in-trigued how group members had different ideas about what was okay, when it came to dealing with children's challenging behaviour.

Martin thought a quick smack was fine if his child was acting out. Mau-reen was adamant that this was never okay. They asked Joy her opinion. She suggested they do a quick activity.

'Imagine you are about ten years old. What thoughts enter your head when you hear the word discipline? What symbol would you draw to capture the word discipline?

Draw a symbol or write the first five words or phrases which come into your head.'

They were quiet for a few moments as they drew, and then Joy asked them to share their images.

Trish, like Martin, had drawn a wooden spoon.

Maureen held up her paper with a large open mouth. 'My dad was al-ways shouting,' she explained.

Tom had drawn a shut door. 'Whenever there was any upset I was sent to my room.' Claire's drawing was a hand because she was smacked.

For some it was a picture of a stick - a punishment often inflicted in schools before the laws were changed.

'How did that experience make you feel?' asked Joy.

'I felt nobody understood - or cared,' sighed Trish. 'I wanted to run away.'

'Being punished made me angry,' said Tom. 'I was sent to my room and told to "think about it". All I thought about was how I'd get even with my little brother later.'

'Yes, I used to feel so frustrated. It wasn't fair,' added Maureen. 'I never got to tell my side of the story.'

'One night when I was a kid, we'd got into trouble with my dad and he'd sent the three of us to bed. I told my brother and sister Dad was the silliest fool in the whole world. I didn't realise he was standing outside the door - then I really got it!' laughed Martin.

Although Martin's story sounded funny, Trish realised the punishment must have caused him pain and humiliation.

'So,' asked Joy, 'Did those experiences help you learn?'

'It helped me learn not to get caught!' said Martin.

Trish realised that as children they had often been controlled through fear.

'It makes sense the word discipline conjures negative images, because those were often our childhood experiences,' said Joy. 'But the examples you gave were punishment, not discipline. Punishment evokes fear and humiliation. It triggers the reptlilian brain. It's not going to cause the child to think about the situation in a helpful way. Our parents did the best they knew how, but for many of them punishment was the only way they knew to deal with power struggles and limit setting.'

'So discipline and punishment are different?' asked Pam.

'Punishment and discipline are not the same thing,' replied Joy. 'Punishment tries to control from the outside in. Discipline encourages control from the inside out.'[20]

The Difference Between Punishment and Discipline

Discipline, to ensure boundaries are respected, needs to be part of every home - but punishment leaves negative impressions. Punishment gives a message, 'You are only loved if you do as you are told. You are only of worth if you comply.' Every one of us, no matter how old or young, needs to know we are loved just for who we are. Living in relationship is part of our DNA. Without love and attention, life loses its meaning. We need the love and affirmation of others.

Perhaps you resort to grumbling or use some form of punishment in an attempt to stop a behaviour which annoys you. At a subconscious level, it is possible your child would rather be grumbled at, shouted at or even physically hurt than be ignored. We all need attention and for many children even negative attention feels better than no attention. But punishment doesn't build meaningful connection between parent and child, and it erodes the child's sense of self-worth. Besides this, punishment triggers emotional flooding, which means the child won't learn from the experience, because the reasoning part of the brain will disengage when the child feels fear or shame.

What's more helpful is to use discipline. When you use FLAC you don't disempower your child. If you're careful to give appropriate consequences, he will sense the fairness of it. Your child has a choice so he doesn't feel disempowered. When you HALT be SURE before you use FLAC, feelings of anger or frustration are going to dissipate. When the family energy isn't focused on the negative spinoff of punishment, you will create the firm boundaries as well as the connection you and your family all need to thrive.

Whilst one discipline incident may cause a reaction, over time effective discipline nurtures connection and mutual respect between you and your child.

♡

Joy invited them to take a quiet moment at the close of the session. 'Imagine your children as adults reflecting on their memories of discipline.

What memories will your children have?
What will it take for you to achieve this?
Why does this matter?'

As Trish and Pam travelled home that evening they discussed their new awarenesses.

'I always perceived discipline and punishment to be the same thing. But they are WAY different.'

'Yeah,' said Pam, 'I see now, punishment is always going to create a fear-based reaction. It's going to trigger the reptilian part of the child's brain.'

'And then they'll react. We think we're helping them to learn but zero learning will take place - except how not to get caught next time! I can see how punishment tries to control from the outside in, whereas discipline is encouraging an inside - out response,' said Trish.

'Yeah, inside out makes sense if you want your child to develop self-discipline,' replied Pam. 'Let's buddy on this, so we can figure out FLAC; it's challenging to think of alternatives that I'll follow through.'

'Yes,' said Trish. 'I want to make this a priority. Discipline - not punishment. No wonder my kids got frustrated - I was ignoring their experience! I don't want my children to stifle their anger, like I had to. When I use FLAC I can set limits without breaking connection with my children.'

'Yes,' said Pam. 'And my child's view of herself is going to be affected by her experience with me as parent. So I need to respect her experience. And I need to respect myself too. If discipline is about control from the inside out then I need to first think about my self-discipline.'

'All discipline starts with self.' Tony Humphreys

Before you impose a limit on your child, HALT and be SURE concerning your part in the situation. Ask yourself:
'What is my child's behaviour trying to tell me?'
'What can I choose to do differently?'
'What is needed right now?'

TO SUM UP

In this chapter we've discussed how discipline is different from punishment and why that matters. Discipline matters if you want to raise children who can behave response-ably (i.e. able to respond) rather than be controlled by a fear-based reactivity. Discipline matters if you want your children to know there are other options than coercion or violence to deal with challenging issues in life. Discipline matters if you want a more peaceful home. Discipline matters if you want to raise competent children who have an inner compass to make wise decisions.

As a parent, moving from where you are to where you want to be might seem a daunting journey.

'The journey of a thousand miles starts with a single step.'

Lao-Tzu

You're trying to figure it all out and at times you might feel overwhelmed or discouraged, but, rather than focusing on the isolated upset, notice ways in which home life is going well. In our final chapter we'll look at an interesting concept, which in challenging times can help you to keep heading in the direction you want, so you create the enjoyable and fulfilling experience you want your family life to be.

CHAPTER NINE

Being the Parent You Want to Be

- when the rubber hits the road

Being the Parent You Want to Be
- when the rubber hits the road

♡

Trish couldn't believe it was the last evening of the course. A few weeks ago the people in this room had been strangers and now they seemed a family. She looked round the room. Jim, who had been so shy initially, now chatted freely. Martin, the taxi driver, who'd been friendly from the beginning, was the one who brought some of the most challenging thoughts into the group. She and Pam had grown so much closer as they journeyed each week, sharing about how the week had gone and reflecting on the evening's discussion as they travelled home after the course.

She appreciated how Joy encouraged them to notice what was working; to develop the art of 'listening to their children's behaviour'. Trish recognised she'd become so much more aware of how she parented. When her children reacted or responded she could think about her part in it.

Joy's voice jolted her into the room:

'It's our last night together,' said Joy. 'Who would be willing to share a key awareness you have gained through the course?'

There was quiet for a few seconds.

'Think cooperation - win-win,' remarked Martin, always quick to jump into conversation.

'Choose to be in 'Approach' mode,' added Maureen. 'And put on your own oxygen mask before you try to help others.'

'Focus on developing competent kids, rather than compliant kids,' said Maeve. 'Even though it's not always easy.'

'HALT, be SURE before you use FLAC - so you can create a discipline approach that works,' said Trish.

'I've realised my child feels a whole lot more secure if he knows where the boundaries are,' said Pam.

'FLAC's working for us,' added Trish. 'I'm not nagging and shouting anymore because FLAC has given me a clear direction to take when the kids test the limits. Home is calmer and happier now.'

'Yes,' said Martin. 'Learning about the crocodile brain was huge for me. I'm recognising when I'm losing the cool now, and most of the time I can reengage my thinking brain and respond rather than react. Even if I do react, afterwards I can figure out what happened, rather than blame the kids for making me mad, or beat myself up for losing my cool.'

'The one thing I'm noticing,' added Trish, 'before I did the course, I got frustrated with my kids but now I'm getting frustrated with myself.'

Joy laughed. 'That makes sense,' she said, 'because you're at a higher level of skill now.'

Trish looked puzzled.

'Let me explain,' said Joy.

The Conscious Competence Model

Like Trish, you may recognise greater awareness about parenting means your frustration with your child lessens, because you've become aware his behaviour makes sense, even if it isn't always convenient or comfortable. Rather than putting your energy into trying to stop the behaviour you don't like, you've become mindful to figuring out what's really going on.

You've also become more aware of how your behaviour impacts family interactions. You're trying to keep balance between your agenda and theirs. Sometimes your kids push your buttons. You don't always have the support you need to provide the affirming emotional climate you know your children need. You're thinking you're not the parent you want to be. When you disappoint yourself by not taking their viewpoint into consideration, when you don't plan ahead adequately to accommodate everyone's needs, when you don't slow down to listen - you get frustrated with yourself. The task of Parenting can feel overwhelming. You may experience this more as you become increasingly aware of how great an impact your way of being has within the Parenting situation. Knowing more about what is needed and what is helpful can seem as stressful as learning to drive. This isn't a bad thing. Your frustration with yourself is a sign you're moving to a higher level of parenting competence. It's actually good news!

This is where you'll find the 'Conscious Competence' model helpful.[21]
There are four skill stages:
a. Unconsciously Unskilled
b. Consciously Unskilled
c. Consciously Skilled
d. Unconsciously Skilled

Let's look at each stage. Notice your level of increasing competence.

a. Unconsciously Unskilled

When I was a younger, less aware parent, (and confident I had all the answers I needed), I thought I was doing fine in my parenting.
I was in a stage of Unconsciously Unskilled. I remember older, wiser friends, who were also parents, telling me about the fabulous Parenting course they were attending. I could not figure why they would join a programme like that and I was dismissive of their enthusiasm. I figured, as a qualified teacher, I knew how to handle children, until some years later my second son's frequent reactive behaviour towards me let me know something wasn't okay.
To paraphrase Maya Angelou,
'You're doing the best you can right now, and when you know better you'll do better.'[22]
At this stage of Unconsciously Unskilled, it's easy to blame your child (or your spouse!) when things go wrong, rather than reflecting on what you could do differently; what would be more helpful and create a more harmonious outcome. To compare this phase of my Parenting with potty training, being Unconsciously Unskilled is like a toddler filling his pants and being unaware of this.

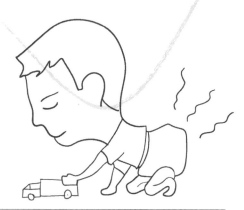

---

21 HTTP://WWW.GORDONTRAINING.COM/FREE-WORKPLACE-ARTICLES/LEARNING-A-NEW-SKILL-IS-EASIER-SAID-THAN-DONE/ 02/11/2014
22 HTTP://WWW.GOODREADS.COM/AUTHOR/QUOTES/3503.MAYA_ANGELOU 12 OCTOBER 2014

b. Consciously Unskilled

As I became more aware I developed more understanding and skills to connect in a helpful way to my children, I became Consciously Unskilled. I was becoming increasingly aware when I parented in an unhelpful way. I was learning to listen to my children's behaviour, instead of trying to manage it. This increased my parenting awareness; I questioned myself about what might be going on in the situation and to develop new skills. At this point of Consciously Unskilled, it required a great deal of focus and determination on my part. The support and encouragement of others was also important at this stage, because this is a time when it's easy to fall back into old, less helpful parenting behaviours and thoughts. I focused on my long-term goal of what I did want to achieve. In other words, not to focus on the particular unhelpful incident today but to keep in mind the long-term goal of what really mattered. If I wanted my children to grow to be kind and competent adults, then my everyday interactions with them in the little things mattered. I needed to model kind competency and show by my actions that I perceived my children as kind and competent. These were all part of creating the environment which would achieve the long term success I wanted for my children.

Developing new ways of seeing things, new ways of interacting and different behaviours often felt strange and uncomfortable at this stage. Sometimes it felt awkward, like when I was learning to drive. I was at the 'L' plate stage and it took conscious effort to develop new skills.

Sometimes, when I was learning to connect and respond, rather than react, I felt false because these new skills felt so alien. I was tempted to revert to old patterns. Yes, there were moments of triumph when I saw how a new and different approach created a different result but it also felt daunting: 'Would I ever get a handle on this?'

I focused on what I wanted to achieve and reminded myself of the principles I wanted to embrace. This helped me to keep going when I felt despondent, self-blaming or critical.

At the Consciously Unskilled stage you may sometimes question your ability to parent helpfully. Knowing these thoughts and sensations at this stage are normal can help you to move through this uncomfortable phase. Self-questioning is an indication you are well on the journey. You are not going to parent perfectly - imperfection is part of our humanity. The school system conditioned us we must have everything right and not make mistakes. But making mistakes is how we learn what doesn't work and what does.

As Joy mentioned, you might notice you are frustrated with yourself, rather than frustrated with your children. Congratulations! This is a sign you are more aware in your parenting. Give yourself the same loving support and kindness you give your children as they develop new skills.

Sometimes you may be so focused on the times you 'got it wrong' you overlook the ways in which you helpfully connect with your children. When you focus on what is working within your parenting, you create a more positive frame of mind which helps you stay calm and responsive. This stage of Consciously Unskilled is like the toddler who doesn't always make it to the toilet in time, but he's conscious this is the goal. He needs encouragement and support to affirm he's getting there!

c. Consciously Skilled

Over time I became Consciously Skilled in my parenting approach. Like learning to drive, I knew what I needed to do, but I had to concentrate to achieve it.

During this phase it is important you have the support of like-minded peers, to help you consolidate your new learning and awarenesses. It does not mean your child will be angelic, although relationships will become more cooperative. When you have times of conflict you will have the tools and awareness to turn these from survive to thrive moments. When you don't handle things the way you want to, you now have the awareness to reflect on what you could do differently, which will be more helpful. You are likely to see the link between when you are in attack or avoid mode and your child's reaction. You'll figure out what you need to remain in approach mode, even if it is as simple as taking a moment to focus on your breath, so you respond rather than react. This is like the toddler who's now making it to the toilet most of the time. He's well on the road to competence.

d. Unconsciously Skilled

This stage is when you have mastered the skills, without having to think about each part of the process. At the stage of Unconsciously Skilled in your parenting, this approach and the new skills you've acquired are now a regular part of life, and you can't imagine it being otherwise.

This is like the child who can now take responsibility for his own toileting.

Over time I have moved into Unconsciously Skilled when I am facilitating a Parenting course - well most of the time. There are times when I'm modelling a skill, I get feedback,

'Oh - and you also did such-and-such.'

'Did I?' I responded.

The skill flowed so naturally, I wasn't aware of it.
This is like driving competently along the highway, hardly aware of the skills you are using.

Making Sense of the 'Stages of Competence' from a Parenting Perspective

What's helpful about knowing these stages is you can recognise where you are. In particular, you can be aware of your own feelings and thoughts at this stage and recognise how these are normal.

You will feel frustrated some of the time, but, as we mentioned earlier, with greater awareness, who you are frustrated with changes. When I was Unconsciously Unskilled I cruised along in blissful ignorance, with occasional bouts of frustration at my 'uncooperative' or 'bratty kids'. Now I'm aware, at a more conscious level of competence, I find the frustration is with myself.

That makes sense when you recognise feelings of frustration are a signal that change is needed. In earlier days, I blamed my children or hubby, now I recognise the only person I can change is myself. The way I choose to be in any situation impacts the outcome.

If you are 'beating yourself up' about parenting incidents you didn't handle well, you increase your stress level. This increases the cortisol levels in your body, which makes it more likely you will react. The cortisol fires the 'crocodile brain', which makes it difficult to think clearly and be the parent you want to be. This is why it is important you are kind and encouraging towards yourself (also known as 'self-compassion'). When you are a relaxed parent who takes time for fun and relaxation, you have more endorphins in your system. These 'feel good' chemicals suppress the cortisol, which means the crocodile brain calms, so instead of reacting you choose a reasoned whole brain engaged response.

♡

'It's hard to be kind to myself, when I realise I've reacted and ignored all I've been learning,' commented Mauren.

Joy nodded, then asked the group,
'So who do you think is the better juggler - the juggler who can juggle
three balls or the juggler who can juggle seven balls?'
They laughed and looked puzzled.
It was clear the juggler juggling more balls is more skilled.
'Now ask yourself, who do you think has dropped more balls?'
'It's pretty obvious - the juggler who's juggling more balls,' said Mau-
reen.
'Exactly,' said Joy. 'He's made more errors in the process of learning
his skill. We make mistakes when we learn new things. We're going to
make mistakes in the learning process. That's the way we learn!'

Making mistakes is a natural part of the growing and learning process -
for yourself as parent as well as for your children.

Your skill level determines what you will give attention to.[23] If you are
stuck in the rut of a low level of skill, you focus on the nit-picking
stuff, rather than deal with the key issue. When the parenting task is
challenging, ask yourself 'What really matters here?' Focus on the big
picture and your long-term goal of raising a competent child. In this
way you stretch yourself into a higher level of skill.

When your kids, or other family members, push your buttons you
sometimes fall back into your old default mode - the modus operandi
you have used for so many years. It takes conscious determination to
choose a different, more helpful way to handle a situation. Sometimes
things get worse before they get better.

'During any transition, performance will inevitably decline before
reaching the improved desired state.' Schneider Goldwasser [24]

The family was used to you as you were - they knew what behaviour
to expect from you. Don't be surprised now they test you: 'Are you
for real?'

Be conscious of how you parent, and how you choose to be in
relationships. It matters. And it matters most in challenging times.

23 BURCHARD 2012:62
24 BRUBAKER AND ZIMMERMAN 2009: P57

When things aren't easy in the home is when you need to have already learnt the skills to negotiate the difficult patches.

It's similar to driving. My husband and I grew up in a subtropical climate. When we moved to Ireland and experienced our first snowy weather I avoided driving, feeling uncertain how to handle the unfamiliar, slippery conditions. My husband took a different approach. First he ventured out on the quiet roads in our suburb, getting a feel of how the steering and brakes reacted.

'Why are you driving in this when you don't have to?' I queried.

'I'll have to drive in snow sooner or later,' he explained. 'So I'm using this opportunity to learn how to handle the car in these conditions. Right now it's easy for me to get a feel for how to do this, even though it's unfamiliar. I don't want to wait till I have to handle a snow storm before I learn what's needed!'

It's like that with Parenting. When an emotional emergency arises, you'll want to already have the insights, the skills and the confidence to steer your family through the situation. There's no time like the present to develop your skill as a parent.

And, like planning a journey, you need to know where you're going. Your clear sense of where you're headed will guide you in the moment by moment decisions. Sometimes you'll need to backtrack, to make a U-turn, to plan a new course, to make the changes which bring your vision into reality. That's okay. Life is like that.

There will be times when you disappoint yourself. That's okay too because you get the opportunity to model the art of apologising and your child will learn humans don't always choose the helpful option and relationships can be repaired.

What do you want your child to learn from your example?

As you model a respectful approach to relationship it is caught by the other family members, including your child.

'Wonder and love are caught not taught;
and to catch them we must be in an atmosphere where we are sure to
find the germs.' Evelyn Underhill

Like our winter colds, the 'respect contagion' will spread itself around the family. Respect and caring are viral. Family members will catch a more respectful, enquiring approach to their interactions when they're exposed to it.

♡

Trish stopped the car outside Pam's door.

'Can you believe we've finished!' she exclaimed.

Pam shook her head. 'I feel I'm a different person than the one who walked out this door six weeks ago,' she said.

'It's going to be hard without the group support. Coffee at 'The Pigsback' next Tuesday?'

Her friend grinned and nodded. Even their latte time together would be different now.

Trish pecked her on the cheek and gave her a hug.

'Thank you.' They both knew this was just the beginning.

As Trish pulled out the driveway she felt a tear slide down her cheek. She smiled. Sad the course had finished. Happy, even though she might not know what lay ahead, she knew how to handle the journey.

♡

CONCLUSION

In this final section we've reflected on the journey from Unconsciously Unskilled (when you haven't got a clue where you're going or how you are going to get there), through Consciously Unskilled and Consciously Skilled to Unconsciously Skilled, (where you know what direction you are headed and what essentials are needed for the journey).

I hope the experience of Trish and the other parents has encouraged you.

You're the parent. You can choose to HALT, be SURE before you use FLAC. By taming your crocodile and choosing Approach mode, you can raise competent children. You can create the environment for your family to think more clearly, connect more compassionately and behave more response-ably, so you live more joyfully.

In each situation ask yourself,

'What matters here? What really matters?'

Imagine the possibilities in our homes,
in our education systems,
in our communities,
in our world,
when each one of us chooses to be the parent we want to be.

'You, and only you, possess total knowledge of, and capacity to create, your right life.' Martha Beck

Bibliography

Brubaker & Zimmerman (2009) *Healthy Organizations*, Goodbooks, USA

Burchard, Brendon (2012) *The Charge*, Free Press, New York

Humphreys, Tony (1998) *A Different Kind of Discipline*, Newleaf, Dublin

Jampolsky, Gerald and Cirincione, Diane (2008) *Finding Our Way Home*, Hay House, Cornwall

Juul, Jesper (1995) *Your Competent Child*, Farrar, Straus & Giroux, New York

Louv, Richard (2008) *Last Child in the Woods: Saving Our Children from Nature-deficit Disorder*, Atlantic Books, New York

Love, Patricia and Stosny, Steven (2007) *Why Women Talk and Men Walk*, Vermilion, London

Roth, Geneen (2010) *Women, Food and God*, Simon and Schuster, London

Scott Peck (2008) *The Road Less Travelled – A New Psychology of Traditional Values and Spiritual Growth*, Random House Group, Great Britain

Siegel, Daniel and Hartzell, Mary (2004) *Parenting from the Inside Out – How a Deeper Understanding Can Help You Raise Children Who Thrive*, Jeremy P. Tarcher - Penguin, New York

Silk, Danny (2008) *Loving Our Kids on Purpose*, Destiny Image Publishers, Inc., Shippensburg, USA

Sunderland, Margot (2007) *The Science of Parenting*, Dorling Kindersley, London

be

before you use

copyright©ValMullally

THANK YOU FOR READING!

Dear Reader

I hope you enjoyed **'BEHAVE – What To Do When Your Child Won't'** and I trust it has given you helpful insights and practical tips to create a calmer, happier family life. Many readers are asking me, 'What's next, Val?' If you'd like to keep in the loop as to what other resources we have available or will be publishing soon, please sign up for our newsletter on http://www.behave.ie.

As an author I love feedback, because it helps me make my work more meaningful for parents and practitioners. We are living in a wonderfully technological age, where you, the reader, has the power to influence discourse and have a say in how future books are written. Please do take the opportunity to let your voice be heard by contacting me directly at val@koemba.com, via the website or writing a review. Whether this book was just what you'd hoped for or if I need to hear some constructive criticism, please let me know what you think.
and what you'd like to read more about.
You can also connect with me on @valmullally on Twitter. Please use the hashtag #BEHAVEbook if you're wanting to share conversations about the book.

If you'd be willing to do so, I'd love you to give a review of this book. Your review not only guides my writing but also informs other readers as to whether this will be helpful for them, so please pop across to my Amazon Author page and leave an honest review.

Thank you for reading 'BEHAVE- What To Do When Your Child Won't' and for spending time with me.

With gratitude

Val Mullally

P.S. Please remember I'm available as a Keynote Speaker re the Koemba Parenting approach, supporting families to:
* think more clearly
* connect more compassionately
* behave more response-ably and live more joyfully.

79460079R00065

Made in the USA
Columbia, SC
24 October 2017